Trauma of Women with Substance Use Disorders

TABLE OF CONTENTS

CHAPTER 1

INTRODUCTION

Introduction to the Study

This chapter provides an introduction to this study that examines the relationship between trauma and spiritual well-being of women with substance use disorders. Further, the chapter includes: the background of the study, the statement of the problem and justification for the study, the purpose and research questions, the definition of terms, the theoretical rationale of the study, and a brief summary of the chapter.

Background of the Study

The Prevalence and Impact of Substance Abuse on Society

Based on criteria from the Diagnostic and Statistical Manual of Mental Disorders, 4th edition (DSM-IV), an estimated 22.5 million Americans are classified with a substance use disorder (Substance Abuse and Mental Health Services Administration, 2010). Of these, 3.2 million Americans are classified with a substance use disorder that includes both alcohol and illicit drugs (Substance Abuse and Mental Health Services Administration, 2010). Substance use disorders are the most commonly diagnosed psychiatric disorder in the United States (Compton, Thomas, Stinson, & Grant, 2007).

Estimates of the overall costs of substance use disorders within the United States measured by diminished vocational and educational productivity, unemployment, domestic violence, child abuse, family disintegration, alcohol related accidents, rising medical costs, crime, and children born with substance related complications, exceeds $600 billion annually. This includes $181 billion for illicit drugs, $193 billion for tobacco and $235 billion for alcohol (National Institute on Drug Abuse, 2011). As staggering as these numbers are, they do not fully describe the breadth of the destructive public health and safety implications of substance use disorders.

Reduction of Resources for Substance Abuse Services

While public concern regarding the influence of substance use continues to intensify, addressing the increasing demand and complexities of substance use disorders is challenging for a variety of reasons. First, as the demand for treatment services increases, available resources decrease (SAMHSA, 2011). In 2011, an estimated 21.6 million persons age twelve or older needed treatment for an illicit drug or alcohol problem. Of these, 2.3 million (less than one percent) received treatment at a substance abuse treatment facility. Thus, 19.3 million persons needed treatment for a substance use problem but did not receive the care needed (SAMHSA, 2011). When treatment is available, individuals seeking treatment are faced with long waiting lists and abbreviated lengths of treatment (Najavits, Schmitz, Gotthardt, & Weiss, 2005).

Second, the magnitude of co-occurring clinical exigency has expanded the scope of care and necessitated comprehensive integration of services. Third, emerging evidence has underscored significant gender differences in substance-related epidemiology; social factors and characteristics; biological response; progression to dependence; medical consequences; co-occurring psychiatric disorders; history of victimization and violence; and barriers to treatment entry, retention, and completion (Kauffman, Silver, & Poulin, 1997; Najavits, 2002; SAMHSA, 2011; Tuchman, 2010). While the reasons for these differences continues to be explored, clinical practice has challenged existing treatment models and community supports which are based on male-normed theoretical perspective, clinical symptomtology and service delivery systems (Kauffman, et al.,, 1997; Najavitis, et al., 2005; Tuchman, 2010).

Gender and Substance Abuse

Epidemiologic Data

The epidemiology of women's substance use outlines the unique risks and challenges which influence the derivation, diagnosis, progression, and provision of treatment services for women with substance abuse disorders (National Institute of Health, 1999; SAMHSA, 2011; Tuchman, 2010). Awareness of gender specific patterns of substance use provides a crucial framework for understanding the nature of those risks and challenges (Tuchman, 2010).

Adult men are more likely than adult women to be alcohol users (65.9% verses, 57.9%), and illicit substance abusers (10.5 % versus 6.2%; Substance Abuse and Mental Health Services Administration, 2006; Tuchman, 2010; Westermeyer & Boedicker, 2000). However, women exhibit greater use of prescription medications (Kauffman, Silver, & Poulin, 1997), and are more likely to abuse multiple substances (Bloom & Covington, 1998; Kauffman, et al., 1997). Furthermore, women are more likely to combine prescription drug abuse with marijuana, cocaine, or other drugs (U.S. Department of Health and Human Services, 2003).

Women's use of cocaine and opiates continue to increase at rates that are analogous to men (Brady & Ashley, 2005). However, women tend to initiate cocaine use earlier than men (Kosten, Kosten, & McDougle, 1996). They are more likely to become regular users of cocaine after a shorter period of time and report ephemeral periods of abstinence (White, Brady, & Sonne, 1996).

According to Emslie, Lewars, Batty and Hunt (2009) and Orwin, Francisco, and Bernichon (2001), retrospective reports from individuals diagnosed with alcohol dependence reveal that women consume smaller amounts of alcohol and are less likely to drink daily or to engage in binge patterns of alcohol use. Women are more likely to describe the onset of substance use as sudden and heavy, while men often describe their substance use as gradual (Westermeyer & Boedicker, 2002; Westermeyer & Boedicker, 2002).

Progression to Dependence

The progression or developmental stages of substance use disorders differs between genders. While men evidence higher rates of substance use disorders across time, the proportion of females with substance use disorders has increased over the past decade (Blumenthal, 1998; SAMHSA, 2011). Women represent approximately one-third of the estimated fourteen million alcohol abusing and dependent individuals in the United States (Brady & Ashley, 2005). Research supports a more rapid presentation of addictive symptomatology and an expedited course to addiction for women (Najavits, 2004; Westermeyer & Boedicker, 2000). These findings have led to the theory of "telescoping". Telescoping means that for women, the time from first intoxication, to alcohol dependence is shorter than men (Najavits, 2005; Sugarman, DeMartini, & Carey, 2009; Tuchman, 2010). This accelerated course to substance dependence underscores the unique biological responses and widespread medical complications of women with substance use disorders.

Biological Response & Medical Consequences

Biological indicators show gender specific metabolic and physiological expressions of substance use (Thomason, 1985; Tuchman, 2010). Women experience heightened levels of intoxication after drinking smaller quantities of alcohol and sustain higher blood alcohol concentrations (Mumenthaler, et al., 1999; Sugarman, et al., 2009). Similarly, women display unique biological responses to cocaine use (Tuchman, 2010). Although women initiate cocaine use sooner and have a more rapid course to addiction (Kosten, et al., 1996), women report diminished levels of euphoria and dysphoria compared to men (Lucas, Angulo, Moal, McEwen

& Piazza, 1998). Administered identical doses of cocaine, men and women experience the equivalent cardiovascular responses despite the fact that blood concentrations of cocaine did not rise as high in women. Furthermore, Tuchman (2010) found that women and men showed similar impairment in tests of concentration, memory, and academic achievement following sustained abstinence, even though women had greater use of cocaine.

Adverse medical consequences occur more rapidly in women who abuse substances than in males who consume similar quantities. In fact, just two drinks a day puts women at risk for physical illness, while for men five drinks a day place them at similar risk (Greenfield, Brooks, Gordon & Green, 2007). These increased risks are attributed to the influence of the metabolism of alcohol in the stomach, hormone levels, reduced amounts of water in women's bodies, and increased concentrations of body fat. Because the alcohol content is more concentrated, it potentiates more expansive damage to bodily organs (Gomberg and Nirenberg, 1993). Studies confirm higher rates of liver problems, hypertension, anemia, gastrointestinal disorders, cognitive impairment, breast cancer, pancreatitis, cardiovascular problems, and physical injury in women verses male alcohol abusers (Diehl, 2002; Loft, Olesen, & Dossing, 1987; NIAAA, 2001; Schenker, 1997; Thurman, 2000; Tuchman, 2010). Additionally, research reveals that acute and chronic alcohol exposure weakens the body's immune response (Kovacs & Messingham, 2002). Suppression of the immune response impedes the ability of white blood cells to migrate to sites of injury and inhibits infection fighting capabilities necessary for healing (Kovacs & Messingham, 2002).

Furthermore, women who experience substance use disorders encounter gynecologic reproductive difficulties such as infertility, changes to menstruation and ovulation, vaginal infections, recurring miscarriages, and premature menopause, (Blume, 1998). Substance abuse is the most widespread problem in high-risk pregnancies (Diehl, 2002; Thurman, 2000; Woods, 1998). Furthermore, many women in substance abuse treatment report an association between their menstrual cycles and incidence of substance use relapse (Covington & Surrey, 1997).

Women's substance use is also associated with sexual dysfunction. Covington and Surrey (1997) found that sexual dysfunction was the single best predictor of women's alcohol problems over a five year period. The use of substances to increase sexual responsiveness, and satisfaction is common. Patterned use of substances to alleviate apprehension associated with sexual engagement and expression can foster addiction as this pattern gets entrenched over time (Gomberg and Nirenberg, 1993). Similarly, the interplay of gender-specific drug use patterns creates environments in which women are more vulnerable to high-risk sexual practices (shared paraphernalia with an injection partner, exchange sex for money or drugs, and difficulty negotiating condom use with sexual partners). These behaviors increase the incidence of sexually transmitted diseases, unwanted pregnancy, and infection with the human immunodeficiency virus (HIV; Tuchman, 2010).

During the past decade, new HIV cases decreased among men but increased among women. In fact, women represent the fastest growing group of new HIV cases. Sixty-five percent of women who get HIV contract it from injection drug use or sexual contact with someone who injects drugs (Blumenthal, 1998; Tuchman, 2010). Furthermore, acquired immune deficiency syndrome (AIDS) is the third leading cause of death in women of reproductive age and the first among African American women (Selwyn, 1998).

Women who abuse substances are more likely than men to attempt suicide (Blume, 1997). Similarly, women are twice as likely to die from substance related problems as men who have the same patterns of consumption (Cook, 2005; McGrady & Raytexk, 1993; Tuchman,

2010). Heightened mortality rates may result from a pattern of avoidance among substance abusing women to contact with the medical community due to the shame associated with their substance use and substance using behaviors. As a result, when they eventually seek medical care they present with more advanced stages of disease (Tuchman, 2010).

Demographic Characteristics of Women with Substance Use Disorders

Several demographic factors differentiate women who have been diagnosed with substance use disorders from to their male counterparts. Each of these characteristics increase risk factors associated with substance use disorders. First, women are more likely than men to come from families where one or more members are addicted to drugs or alcohol (Nelson-Zlupko, Kauffman & Dore, 1995; Tuchman, 2010; White, Brady, & Sonne, 1996). This dynamic often accompanies familial expectations, directed toward the women in the family, to manage heighted levels of familial and financial disruptions (Tuchman, 2010).

Second, women are more likely to be in relationships with drug-abusing partners (Bloom & Covington, 1998; Kauffman, Silver, & Poulin, 1997; Tuchman, 2010; US Department of Health and Human Services, 2011). Similarly, data suggests that women are more likely to initiate and maintain use in their intimate relationships (Kauffman, et al, 1997; Tuchman, 2010). In fact, women are more likely to attribute the initiation and continuation of their substance abuse to environmental and relational stressors (Kauffman, et al., 1997; Nelson-Zlupko, et al, 1995).

Third, women are more likely to work in the home and fulfill primary childcare responsibilities (Westermeyer & Bodicker, 2000). Concerns regarding childcare issues and fears that if substance abuse issues are exposed, their children will be removed from the home often hinders the exploration and integration of appropriate intervention and care (Tuchman, 2010).

Additionally, treatment entry for men is often initiated by an employer or the criminal justice system, whereas for women treatment entry is often the result of a social work referral or the recommendation of a social service agency (Grella & Joshi, 1999; Tuchman, 2010).

Fourth, women are more likely to report diminished life expectations, have less education, fewer job skills, greater levels of unemployment, and fewer financial resources (Kauffman, et al., 1997). These concerns often limit early detection and intervention for substance abuse and often restrict treatment options (Tuchman, 2010).

Employment is a fundamental life activity that provides income, fosters social relationships, enhances social status, provides time-based structure, promotes a sense of well-being and provides a sense of meaning and value for individuals and their families (Leufstadius, Eklund, & Erlandson, 2009; Van Campen & Cardol, 2009). However, the inclusion of vocational evaluation, job training skills, and vocational placement is rarely part of substance abuse treatment programming (West, 2008). When vocational evaluation and skills building are part of a holistic program of care studies reveal improved treatment retention and enhanced treatment outcomes (Adamson, Sellman, & Frampton, 2009; Hogue Dauber, Dasaro, & Morgenstern., 2010; Lidz, Sorrentino, Robison, & Bunce, 2004; Sligar & Toriello, 2007; SAMHSA, 2009, December; Young, 2000; Walls, Moore, Batiste & Loy, 2009; West, 2008).

Fifth, women select different settings for use. Women are more likely to seek private or socially isolated settings for use while men tend to use more public settings. These differences may be reflective of differing levels of social acceptance of substance use of men and women (Kauffman, et al., 1997).

Sixth, Kauffman, et al. (1997) suggests that women view the abuse of substances more negatively than men. As a result women are more likely to express feelings of guilt, shame, and anxiety in relation to their substance use. Internalized guilt, shame, and anxiety restricts self-exploration and integration of treatment.

Seventh, women incarcerated for drug-related offenses represent one of the fastest growing populations in jails and prisons. Women confined to prison increased from 7.8% in 1974 to 10.3% in 2001 (Tuchman, 2010). Reasons for arrest and incarceration include: drug possession; sale of drugs; and crimes committed to support addiction, such as theft or prostitution (Najavits, 2005; Tuchman, 2010; Nelson-Zlupko, et al., 1995). In fact, women are more likely to support their substance use through petty larceny and prostitution, whereas men rely on robbery, con games, and burglary (Kauffman, et al., 1997). Furthermore, half of the incarcerated women surveyed by the Bureau of Justice Statistics reported that they committed their offenses under the influence of drugs or alcohol (U.S. Department of Justice, 1994).

Eighth, homelessness is a growing problem within the United States. Women now represent 32% of the homeless population (Douglas & Jimenez, 2008). In a UCLA Homeless Women's Health Study of 974 women, Arangua, Anderson & Gelberg, (2005) found that homeless women evidence higher rates of substance abuse, mental health problems, and victimization. Similarly, homeless women present with more advanced medical issues. However, utilization rates for mental health, substance abuse, and health related issues are poor (Arangua, Anderson & Gelberg, 2005; Munoz, Crespo & Perez-Santos, 2005).

Integration of gender inclusive and gender-responsive substance abuse treatment is needed to address gender specific barriers that limit access to treatment, impede proactive assessment and treatment intervention, and hinder treatment engagement, retention and completion. The following section provides a review of barriers to treatment for females with substance abuse disorders.

Statement of the Problem and Justification of the Study

Barriers to Treatment

Women seek treatment for substance abuse less often than men (Shober & Annis, 1996; Tuchman, 2010; Weisner & Schmidt, 1992). In 2002, 30% of admissions to substance abuse treatment programs were women (Tuchman, 2010). Low rates of substance abuse treatment entry among women reflect gender specific barriers. These barriers dissuade treatment access, impede treatment retention, and hinder treatment completion (Blume, 1990; Tuchman, 2010).

Social Stigma

Throughout history there have been distinct parameters and regulations for alcohol consumption for men and women. Often, women are faced with greater stigmatization and are judged more harshly for substance use and intoxication (Najavitis, 2005, Taylor, 2010; Wiechelt, 2008). Ancient Roman law made use of alcohol by women illegal, and records show where women were put to death for drinking. In many traditions, drinking is symbolic of an individual's membership or citizenship. Thus, limiting a woman's use of alcohol was representative of a woman's position in societal order (Health, 1993).

Western thought dating back to the ancient Talmud, held that alcohol would lead women to promiscuity. From 1936 to 1958 the U.S. Distilled Spirits Council prohibited the use of women in advertisements for alcoholic beverages. Today, a woman who uses substances faces greater stigmatization than men (Blume, 1990; Tuchman, 2010).

This sense of moral failing combined with the social stigma attached to substance use provides a catalyst for surreptitious use of substances and prompts women to seek relief through ancillary sources such as their medical or mental health provider rather than substance abuse treatment settings (Tuchman, 2010). Often symptoms of substance use are masked by symptoms of depression or medical concerns (SAMHSA, 2011; Weschsberg, Luseno, & Ellerson, 2008). In medical settings, women are less likely to be identified as having substance use disorder than men (Chang, 1997; SAMHSA, 2011). As a result, providers may not detect or diagnose primary substance use thus delaying appropriate referral and intervention (Weschsberg, Luseno, & Ellerson, 2008).

Isolation and Lack of Relationships or Support

As previously discussed, women with substance use disorders are more socially isolated than men. They tend to drink at home in isolation and in private (Tuchman, 2010; Zlupko, Kauffamn, & Dore, 1995). They report having few to no friends and limited social networks (Tuchman, 2010; Nelson-Zlupko, et al., 1995). One study showed that 84 percent of women diagnosed with alcoholism identify drinking at home (Blume, 1997).

Additionally, women entering treatment are less likely to have active treatment supports and receive less emotional support from their partners for entering treatment (Tuchman, 2010). When women enter treatment their partners tend to remain neutral; when men enter treatment their partners tend to be highly supportive. Also, women are more often deserted by a partner for drinking than men (Gomberg & Nirenberg, 1993; Tuchman, 2010). Women are less likely to be encouraged to go to treatment by family members and friends (Beckman & Amaro, 1986; Tuchman, 2010). Often women are discouraged from participating in treatment by family members who perceive their involvement in treatment as a threat to their ability to care for their family (Nelson-Zluko, et al., 1995).

Childcare Issues

Women with substance use disorders have difficulty participating in treatment because they lack childcare for their children (Taylor, 2010; Tuchman, 2010). They tend to be the primary care givers of their children as well as others in their family (Nelson-Zlupko, et al., 1995; SAMHSA, 2011; Tuchman, 2010). For many women, particularly those of lower socioeconomic backgrounds, alternative childcare is unaffordable or unavailable (Colette, 1998; SAMHSA, 2011). Additionally, few drug treatment programs offer on-site childcare or provide help in making child care arrangements. Most residential programs do not allow parents to bring their children to treatment. Zankowski (1987) found the most common reason for women to leave treatment prematurely was due to the needs of dependent children. Many women are discouraged from participating in treatment by a family member who perceives the addicts' involvement in treatment as a threat to her ability to care for the family (Nelson-Zlupko, et al., 1995; SAMHSA, 2011). Many women fear that acknowledging and/or exposure of their substance abuse may lead incarceration or the loss of custody of their children (Beckman & Amero, 1986).

Finances

Women comprise more than half of all individuals living in poverty in the United States (U.S. Department of Agriculture [USDA]). Women with substance use disorders are often single parents with less financial resources. Many are unemployed and cannot afford to pay for treatment. Also women are more likely to drop out of treatment due to financial problems (Beckman & Amaro, 1986). Although federal block grants secure treatment availability for women, there are not enough treatment beds/slots to serve the women in need of services. These women are less likely to have insurance or other economic resources to cover the costs of treatment (Taylor, 2010). Similarly, women are more likely to encounter difficulty with transportation to the treatment sites (Shober & Annias, 1996; Tuchman, 2010).

Programming

Women are often cautious to disclose the extent of, or seek treatment for substance use issues. As a consequence, women remain underrepresented in substance abuse treatment and in substance abuse research (Tuchman, 2010). The majority of substance abuse research and treatment programs are based on male norms (Najavitis, 1997; Tuchman, 2010). As a result, many substance abuse treatment programs fail to adequately assess and address psychodynamic characteristics of women (Weschsberg Luseno, & Ellerson, 2008).

Wilke (1994) asserts that early identification of substance use disorders in women is critical. However, some assessment instruments (Michigan Alcoholism Screening Test [MAST Selizer, 1971]; Addiction Severity Index [ASI], McClellan, et al., 1980; Luborsky, Obrien, & Woody, 1980) reflect a male bias and as a result, they more accurately assess male substance abuse than female substance abuse (Mendelson & Millo, 1998; Wilke, 1994). According to Wilke (1994), women tend to evaluate risks associated with alcohol and drug use as more saliently then men. Such attitudinal differences may constitute false positive or false negatives. Also, instruments that are gender specific with regard to addictive patterns, health consequences, and interpersonal and situational stressors are critical to the identification of substance use disorders among women (Kauffman, et al., 1997).

The complexities of co-occurring issues faced by women with a substance use disorders often lead to fragmentation in clinical care and service delivery. That is, treatment of substance use and mental health disorders are often segregated. This fragmentation leads to delayed detection and intervention, restricted diagnosis, and limited gender specific resources (Najavitis, 1997). Research is expanding knowledge about how to effectively and holistically address the treatment needs of women with substance use disorders. Programs are beginning to integrate gender-responsive, trauma informed and trauma-specific services designed to address the multidimensional concerns of women (Bloom & Covington, 1998; Najavits, 2002; Wechsberg, et al., 2008). Additionally, recent progress includes the adaptation of 12-step programs and other recovery resources for women and the development of new treatments such as women-and children programs (Covington, 2000; Najavits, et al., 2005).

Initial studies found gender responsive and gender-specific addiction treatment services improve treatment completion and abstinence rates (Blume, 1998; Wallen1998; Weiss, 1997), and increased responsiveness to outpatient behavioral treatment (Najavits, 2005). Research also endorses the efficacy of treatment intervention. Findings confirm that women respond better to treatment than men. A national study of individuals with addiction five years after treatment found that women's substance use decreased twice as much as men (SAMHSA, 1998; SAMHSA, 2010). When able to access treatment, women show major decreases in drug use and criminal arrest (SAMHSA, 1998; SAMHSA, 2010).

Co-Occurring Substance Use and Mental Disorders

Women with substance use disorders often have co-morbid psychiatric disorders. In a study of treatment-seeking opiate abusers, the lifetime prevalence of psychiatric co-morbidity was more than twice as common in women as compared to men (Broomer, King, Kidorf, Schmidt, & Bigelow, 1997; Covington, 2008). More specifically, women with substance use disorders exhibit higher rates of major depression, anxiety disorders, social phobia, post-traumatic stress disorder (PTSD), and eating disorders (Center for Substance Abuse Treatment, 2005; Nelson-Zlupko et al., 1995; Prescott, 2002; SAMHSA, 2011; Tuchman, 2010; Wiechelt, 2008). Often, substances are used to abate symptoms that accompany co-occurring disorders (Center for Substance Abuse Treatment, 2005; Nelson-Zlupko, Wiechelt, 2008; Prescott, 2002;

Tuchman, 2010). Ineffective strategies for managing physical and emotional distress can interfere with treatment engagement and participation and is a frequently cited precipitant for relapse (Tuchman, 2010).

Trauma

Trauma experiences are often at the core of co-occurring substance abuse and mental health issues (Tuchman, 2010). Many women report the initiation of substance use after a specific traumatic event in their lives (Tuchman, 2010; Zlupko, Kauffman, & Dore, 1995). Among women in substance abuse treatment, fifty-five to ninety-nine percent have experienced trauma (Najavits, Weiss, and Shaw, 1997). Trauma is a complex, multifaceted experience which affects all areas of the person; mind, body and spirit and leads to a myriad of long-term consequences, that can be psychological (Denov, 2004; Draucker, 2001; Hall, 1999), physiological (Goldberg & Goldstein, 2000; Golding, 1994; Golding, Cooper & George, 1997), or behavioral (Dimmitt, 1995; Roberts, Reardon & Rosenfeld, 1999; Seng, et.al., 2004).

The diagnostic manual used by mental health providers (DSM IV-TR) defines trauma as, "involving direct personal experience of an event that involves actual or threatened death or serious injury, or other threat to one's physical integrity; or a threat to the physical integrity of another person; or learning about unexpected or violent death, serious harm, or threat of death or injury experienced by a family member or other close associate (American Psychiatric Association [APA] 2000, p. 463). This definition supports that trauma related symptoms can be present in individuals who are directly and indirectly exposed to trauma (Najavatis, 2002). Thus, sources of trauma can include physical abuse, unwanted sexual advances, physical illness, accidents, natural disasters, terrorism, and disruptions in family life (Nelson-Zlupko, et al.,

1995). Traumatic events may be brief, single incidents or prolonged and involve multiple perpetrators (Silver, et al., 2002).

Unwanted sexual advances such as incest and rape are often precipitating traumatic events for drug use among women (Gorden, 2002). In 2006, there were 272,350 reported victims of rape, attempted rape, or sexual assault (Bureau of Justice Statistics, 2003). Rates of sexual and physical abuse reported by women in substance abuse treatment run as high as 75% (Taylor, 2010; Wiechelt, 2008). Childhood sexual abuse affects 27% of female children under the age of eighteen (Finkelhor, Hotaling, Lewis, & Smith, 1990; Taylor, 2010). Prevalence rates for intimate partner violence among women in treatment range between 25% and 57%. However, only thirty-three to fifty-nine percent of women who experience trauma meet diagnostic criteria for posttraumatic stress disorder (PTSD) (Najavits, et al., 1997). In other words, the continuum of trauma (type, duration and multiplicity) often remains unaddressed unless the symptomology meets the explicit criteria for PTSD.

Trauma victims have high rates of anxiety, depression, self-injurious behavior, suicidal impulses, and other behavioral addictions including eating disorders, sexual addictions, and compulsive exercise (Kilpatrick, Resnick, Sanders, & Best, 1998). The bi-directional nature of trauma and addiction predisposes women to greater risks of repeated traumas in the future (Gordon, 2002).

Kendall-Tacket's (2003) review of the literature on the impact of childhood sexual abuse on health, found that trauma survivors report more medical conditions and use medical care at higher rates than the general population. Chronic pain conditions such as fibromyalgia, irritable bowel syndrome, back pain, headaches, pelvic pain, and sleep disorders may have functional rather than organic causes, leading to diagnoses of somatization disorder. Kendall-Tacket (2003) concluded that there is a link between the history of abuse and chronic pain. Connection between interpersonal trauma and somatic symptoms may be particularly important to investigate with older survivors, who often somatize their psychological pain (Higgins & Follette 2002; Krystal, 1991). In addition to somatizing psychological pain, many women will use substances or their spiritual community to cope.

Spirituality and Substance Abuse

Spirituality is "the personal quest for understanding answers to ultimate questions about life, about meaning, and about relationship to the sacred or transcendent, which may (or may not) lead to or arise from the development of religious rituals and the formation of community" (Koenig, McCullough and Larson, 2001, p. 18). The efficacy of spirituality in the treatment and recovery of substance use disorders is widely recognized (Ciarrocchi & Brelsford, 2009; Galanter, Dermatis, Bunt, Williams, Trujillo, & Steinke, 2007; Juhnke, et al., 2009), based in part on the pioneering work of Alcoholics Anonymous (AA), a 12-step mutual support recovery group established in 1935 (Galanter et. al., 2007; Miller, 2002; Miller, 2003). The 12-step model endorses recovery as "a spiritual program" (Miller & Kurtz, 1994), which includes belief in a transcendental being or "higher power" outside of and greater than oneself. Although the nature of the higher power or "God" is intentionally broadly defined in the core literature of AA, the higher power is viewed as a personal and active source of help and hope for those seeking to recover. The successes experienced as a result of the beliefs and practices of AA have contributed to the development of other 12-step recovery programs such as Narcotics Anonymous and Al-Anon (Miller, 2002).

Since it is often in the context of counseling that clients begin to explore issues of spirituality, holistic clinical care seeks to examine and employ intrinsic and existential spiritual resources. Effective implementation of individual faith and spiritual practices can support the attainment of effective coping strategies and mitigate the adverse symptoms that led them to counseling (Aten & Hernandez, 2004; Miller, 2003).

Recognition of the importance of spirituality in the treatment of substance abuse disorders has led to the development of professional organizations focusing on the inclusion of the spiritual dimension in counseling (Aten & Hernandez, 2004; Miller, 2003; Stebnicki, 2006). In fact, the training bodies of several organizations (American Psychological Association [APA]; American Counseling Association [ACA]; Counsel for Accreditation of Counseling and Related Educational Programs, [CACREP]) have specific curriculum requirements in the area of spirituality (Miller, 2003; Stebnicki, 2006). This recognition reinforces holistic clinical incorporation of spirituality throughout the continuum of care. This includes not only substance abuse disorders, but co-occurring disorders including trauma.

Spirituality and Trauma

The experience of and recovery from trauma cannot be understood simply as a cognitive, behavioral, psychological, or sociological encounter. Trauma is also a spiritual experience that necessitates reorganization of the individual's internal value system, worldview, and sense of meaning (Vis & Boynton, 2008). Further, spirituality is a critical component in assisting individuals in moving beyond the immediate impact of trauma by facilitating posttraumatic processing, coping, and symptom management (Vis & Boynton, 2008). Smith (2006) maintains that as individuals recover from trauma, spirituality and trauma become interacting domains. That is, the traumatic event has an impact on the individual's spiritual formation/integration, and on what role spirituality takes in shaping the individual's journey through the trauma. Thus, incorporation of the spiritual dimensions of the traumatized individual's recovery process provides a catalyst for healing and serves as a mitigating factor in reducing post trauma symptomatology (Vis & Boynton, 2008).

Thompson (1985) identifies that spirituality mitigates post trauma symptomatology and promotes recovery in a variety of ways. First, integration of spirituality in trauma recovery assists individuals in reflecting on their beliefs about loss and the process of adjustment. Second, inclusion of spirituality assists individuals in making sense of the experience (why it happened, who-if anyone-is to be held responsible). Third, spirituality helps individuals examine what meaning the event has for their life and in their view of the world. Fourth, spirituality fosters relationship with others through formal and informal support offered in religious and non-religious spiritual communities. Similarly, these communities offer supportive avenues for individuals to talk about and redefine the experience in ways that are more manageable. Harman's (1997) further supports the importance of restoring the connection between survivors and a supportive community. This connection allows for the re-construction of the trauma story in a manner that establishes a sense of internal and external safety. Fifth, the integration of spirituality in trauma recovery allows individuals to identify and include spiritual and religious rituals as part of self-care. These spiritual practices can create a sense of internal awareness, calmness, and safety while generating a sense of manageability of emotions (Vis & Boynton, 2008). It is for these reasons that James Fowler's (1981) faith development theory provides the theoretical underpinnings for the research concerning the relationship between trauma and spiritual well-being of women with substance use disorders.

Theoretical Rationale

Faith Development Theory

In his theory of faith development, Fowler (1981) offers a comprehensive lifespan perspective of spiritual development (Cartwright, 2001). Fowler, contends that levels of spiritual development mark important distinctions in the degrees of complexity with which individuals understand self, the values and commitments that guide them, their relationships and their relationship to the divine (Cartwright, 2001). According to Fowler, spiritual development expands toward progressively more complex levels of understanding, integration, meaning making, and interpersonal relationships (Fowler, 1981; Miller, 2003).

Fowler's (1981) theory is made up of six stages of faith development that mark increased cognitive maturity and personalization of an individual's spiritual "identity" (Green, 2002; Piper, 2004). The stages of faith development are: intuitive-projective faith, mythic-literal faith, synthetic-conventional faith, individuative-projective faith, conjunctive faith, and universalizing faith. In the first stage, intuitive-projective faith, individuals exhibit simplistic cognitive egocentrism. They lack perspective-taking abilities and demonstrate significant dependence on the perceptions of authority figures or past parental messages or storytelling images related to spiritual or religious beliefs. Individuals at this stage of faith development are more concrete and dependent on significant authority figures. They require structure, specific behavioral tasks, and direction from others as support. For example, an individual in early recovery may use the structure of 12-step programming as a way of formulating a concrete plan for recovery. At this stage they seek behaviorally focused direction from their sponsor, and often adopt the core ideas and beliefs of those in their identified recovery group.

In the mysthic-literal faith stage, individuals continue to rely heavily on the guidance of authority figures, but they begin to develop improved capabilities for simple perspective taking and meaning making. However, they lack the ability to fully understand the experiences and beliefs of others. This is exhibited in black-and-white thinking and a strong belief in "right" and "wrong." For example, an individual recovering from a substance use disorder hold rigid conceptualization of twelve step principles. They may struggle with those who have differing ideas or who do not affirm their understanding of the 12-step principles.

Individuals in the synthetic-conventional stage attempt to form a spiritual identity that is integrated into their personal and professional experience. Although they continue to be somewhat rigid and self-focused in their approach to spiritual issues, they exhibit increased social perspective taking abilities and a broader understanding of mutual interpersonal perspectives regarding spirituality. For example, an individual involved in 12-step recovery groups will appreciate the experiences and perspectives of others in the 12-step program, but remain committed to the ideologies presented by their sponsor.

In the individuative-projective faith stage, individuals begin to individuate instead of conforming to the faith of significant others. They critically examine their system of beliefs, symbols, values, and commitments they previously accepted. This analysis is often filled with angst and a sense of confusion particularly when traumatic occurrences experienced contradicts previously held beliefs about others and the divine. However, with guidance and encouragement in a nonjudgmental environment, individuals develop a new sense of spiritual autonomy that allows them to begin to understand the spiritual experiences and meaning making of others in a more expansive way. An individual recovering from substance use disorders maintain their commitment to 12-step principles, but are open to new ideas presented by others in their recovery group.

In the conjunctive faith stage, individuals begin to develop an ability to live with the paradoxical complexities of faith. This fosters their ability to engage in non-defensive, mutual dialogue with those whose traditions differ from their own. Individuals in stage six, universalizing faith, have reached a level of spiritual maturity that promotes a vision for a universal or interconnected community (Fowler, 1981; Fowler & Dell, 2006; Ripley, Jackson, Tatum, & Davis. 2007). For women with co-occurring disorders creating meaning from the experiences and utilizing experiences of others promote a realization of shared experiences with others. This emboldens the creation of a new narrative regarding their experiences.

Purpose and Research Questions

The purpose of this exploratory study is to examine the relationship between trauma and the spiritual well-being in women with substance use disorders. Specifically, this study explored the following research question and sub-questions:

What is the relationship between type of trauma and spiritual well-being, in women with substance abuse disorders when comparing different types of trauma?

Sub-question: (a) What is the relationship between age of first traumatic occurrence and spiritual well-being in women with substance use disorders as measured by the *Spiritual Well-Being Scale* and the *Trauma Assessment*?

Sub-question: (b): What is the relationship between the number of traumatic occurrences and the spiritual well-being in women with substance use disorders as measured by the *Spiritual Well-Being Scale* and the *Trauma Assessment*?

Population Sample and Sampling Procedures

Participants for this study are female residents of a two-year modified therapeutic community in Durham, North Carolina. Participants included in the study met DSM IV criteria for a substance use disorder (SUD). Admission criteria for modified therapeutic community are individuals 18 years or older, having a history of a SUD, being medically and psychiatrically stable, and meeting the American Society of Addiction Medicine (ASAM) criteria for inpatient treatment.

Participant selection for this study utilized a selective sampling method. Selective sampling means participants are deliberately chosen using a sampling plan that included adult females with a history of co-occurring trauma and substance use disorder who met admission criteria for a two-year modified therapeutic community (Heppner, Wampold, & Kivlighan, 2008). A modified therapeutic community refers to a treatment approach that maintains the key elements, structure, and processes of the standard Therapeutic Community model but is designed to accommodate the individual needs, impairments, and deficits of clients with co-occurring disorders (Sacks, Banks, McKendrick & Sacks, 2008).

The use of selective sampling allowed for the inclusion of members of the population that were willing to participate in the study. Support for this sampling method is noted by Serlin (1987) stating, "…valid inference can be made to a hypothetical population resembling the sample" (p. 300).

Definition of Terms

Trauma: The Diagnostic and Statistical Manual of Mental Disorders, Fourth Edition-TR (DSM-IV-TR) defines trauma as, "involving direct personal experience of an event that involves actual or threatened death or serious injury, or other threat to one's physical integrity; or a threat to the physical integrity of another person; or learning about unexpected or violent death, serious harm, or threat of death or injury experienced by a family member or other close associate. The person's response to the event must involve intense fear, helplessness or horror (or in children, the response must involve disorganized or agitated behavior)" (American Psychiatric Association [APA], 2000, p. 463).

Gender-Responsive Services: Gender-responsive services refers to creating an environment through site selection, staff selection, program development, content, and material that reflects an understanding of the lives of women and addresses and responds to their strengths and challenges (Bloom & Covington, 1998).

Trauma-Specific Services: Trauma-specific services refer to the integration of therapy models or interventions that directly address trauma and Posttraumatic Stress Disorder. That is, services designed specifically to address violence, trauma, and related symptoms and reactions. The intent of treatment activities is to increase skills and strategies that allow survivors to manage their symptoms and reactions with minimal disruption to their daily obligations and to their quality of life; and eventually to reduce or debilitating symptoms and to prevent further traumatization and violence (Harris & Fallot, 2001; Najavits & Kanukollu, 2005).

Trauma-Informed Services: Trauma-informed services refer to the education of staff regarding trauma and Posttraumatic Stress Disorder and the inclusion of trauma history as part of comprehensive service provision (Harris & Fallot, 2001; Najavits & Kanukollu, 2005).

Religion: Societal institution phenomenon composed of members who abide by various beliefs and adhere to certain rules, rituals, covenants and formal procedures (Thorensen & Harris, 2002).

Spirituality: Spirituality is "the personal quest for understanding answers to ultimate questions about life, about meaning, and about relationship to the sacred or transcendent, which may (or may not) lead to or arise from the development of religious rituals and the formation of community" (Koenig, McCullough and Larson, 2001, p. 18).

Spiritual Well-Being: A sense of relatedness or connectedness to others, meaning-making and a belief in a relationship with a power higher than self (Imanm, Karim, Jusoh and Mamad, 2009).

Faith: Faith is a "dynamic pattern of personal trust in and loyalty to a center or centers of value. A trust in and loyalty to images and realities of power, trust in and loyalty to a shared master story or core story and having a covenantal structure in which our shared trust transcends us" (Fowler, 1991 p. 92).

Faith Development: Faith development refers to the growth of the individual's capacity to develop a distinct system of beliefs by which he or she finds meaning in life (Fowler, 1981).

Coping: Coping refers to the efforts, both action-oriented and intra-psychic, used to manage environmental and internal demands and conflicts that tax or exceed a person's resources (Lazarus & Folkman, 1984).

Chapter Summary

Chapter one introduced the study by examining the influence of trauma on the spiritual well-being of women with substance abuse disorders. Chapter one contained an overview of the prevalence of substance abuse disorders in the United States; the statement of the problem including gender specific issues related to substance use disorders and gender specific barriers to treatment; a justification for conducting the study; the theoretical basis for the study; outlined the definition of terms used in the study; and the research questions studied. The following chapter will provide a comprehensive review of the theoretical and empirical literature associated with spiritual development theory, trauma theory, and treatment approaches for addressing co-occurring trauma and substance use disorders.

Chapter 2

LITERATURE REVIEW

Introduction to Literature Review

In the preceding chapter, the persistent, pervasive public health and safety implications of substance abuse disorders was established. Further, research reveals gender differences that influence the onset, progression, assessment, treatment accessibility, and scope of intervention. Faith development theory was presented as a framework for examining how trauma impacts the spiritual development of women with co-occurring trauma and substance use disorders. This chapter presents the research on cognitive developmental theory, faith development, trauma informed, and trauma specific approaches to treatment for women with co-occurring trauma and substance abuse disorders.

Faith Development Theory

To date, one of the most influential contributions to the field of faith development has been the research and collective works of James Fowler (Coyle, 2011; Parker, 2006). Fowler (2004) posits a structural paradigm of how faith fluctuates throughout one's lifespan (Devor, 1989; Driedger, 1997). Further, Fowler asserts that faith possesses a recognizable pattern of development across all spiritual experiences. These patterns of faith development are organized into six hierarchal stages that represent progressive shifts in the individual's ability to process, interpret, and individualize complex and often confounding concepts (Fowler, 1981; Miller, 2003). Each stage is measured along seven different, but related, aspects or characteristics of faith (Fowler, 2004; 1991; 1981).

Theoretical Framework of Fowler's Faith Development Theory

Fowler's research reflects the cognitive developmental influences of Jean Piaget's (1967) cognitive development, Lawrence Kohlberg's (1976) theory of moral development, Erik Erikson's (1968; 1980) theory of psychosocial development, and Daniel Levinson's (1978) theory of adult psychosocial development. While each offers domain specific exposition, their collective contributions underscore five distinct and multidimensional assumptions of cognitive developmental theory. First, individuals progress through stages of development that allow them to think and respond in new and more complex ways. Second, stages of growth or change processes are sequential and hierarchal. Individuals move from less complex to greater levels of complex thinking. Third, individuals' growth and stage progression is not inevitable. Individuals' growth and development occur in relationship to environmental interactions. Fourth, there is a consistent relationship between individuals' stage of development and behavioral expressions. Fifth, stage development is culturally universal (McAdams, 1993; Piaget, 1967; Sias, 2002; Sprinthall, 2001).

Consistent with his contemporaries, Fowler's theory offers a structure that outlines faith development in a manner that contains organization, compositional wholeness, hierarchy, and invariant sequentially (Driedger, 1997; Fowler et al., 2004). In contrast to his contemporaries, Fowler expands and reshapes the dimensionality of cognitive developmental theories with the inclusion of multifaceted relational and affective dimensions of spiritual formation and faith development. The affective and theological components reflect the spiritual formation ideologies of comparative historian and religionist Wilfred Cantwell Smith (1962), as well as theologians H. Richard Niebuhr (1951) and Paul Tillich (1952; 1957). Fowler advanced Tillich's idea that faith is not restricted to components of religion, broadened Niebuhr's views regarding the relational qualities of faith, and reinforced Smith's assertion that faith is a universal human experience (Coyle, 2011; Fowler, 1991). Fowler's integration of cognitive developmental theories and spiritual ideologies, initiates operational ways of thinking about faith, how it is shaped, and transformed as individuals grow and mature (Driedger, 1997; Radeck, 2007).

In his later work, Fowler (2004) incorporated the research and gender-specific contributions of Carol Gilligan (1982) and Mary Field Belenky (1986). Their work prompted a re-visioning of developmental theories by highlighting the relational and evolutional distinctions in the moral and spiritual development of women (Astley, 2009; Devor, 1989; Fowler, 1991). Though Belenky (1986) did not ascribe a stage theory of women's development, she highlighted styles of knowing that parallel the developmental stages of Kohlberg (1981), and Fowler (1981). According to Belenky (1986), women give expression to two styles of knowing that impact their faith development. The first expression is a subjective knowing. Subjective knowing includes the development of reflective and critical awareness as well as the testing of one's sense of knowing through objectifying the known and distancing oneself from emotional involvement. The second, procedural knowing precedes a style she calls connected knowing. Belenky (1986) contends that procedural knowing takes place through the development of rapport and proceeds toward self-awareness and critical reflection through, and by way of participation, relation, and the disciplining of subjectivity through dialogue and reflection. Gilligan (1982) and Belenky (1989) assert that relationally based connected knowing is a more distinct and distinguishable aspect of women's' developmental process. Gilligan (1982) further contends that a woman's moral development favors sustaining relational connections defined by care and responsibility over principles and rights. Thus, spiritual development for women is produced and sustained within the context of intrinsic self-awareness and extrinsic integration and ongoing relationship with others (Antley, 2009; Belenky, 1986; Gilligan, 1982).

Definition and Foundation of Fowler's Faith Development Theory

Defining the progression of faith development with the accuracy necessitates a definition that reflects the intricate, dynamic, multifaceted and ultimately ineffable faith process (Driedger, 1997; Fowler, 2004). Fowler's definition of faith has evolved over time. His formal definition of faith, provided in his book, *Stages of Faith* (1986), is as follows:

> "Faith is the process of constitutive-knowing; underlying a person's composition and maintenance of a comprehensive frame (or frames) of meaning; generated from the persons attachments or commitments to centers of superordinate value with power to unify his or her experiences of the world; thereby endowing the relationships contexts, and patterns of everyday life, past, present, and future with significance" (p. 25).

Fowler's definition conveys the complex faucets of faith from many perspectives. First, Fowler (1986) acknowledges the fundamental, yet transitory nature of faith. He maintains that individuals are endowed at birth with the capacity for faith. The assimilation and maturation of faith is uniquely personal and is necessary for sustaining life.

Second, Fowler (2004) contends that faith is more than the simple act of trust. Dynamic faith is so uniquely universal that it transcends religious symbols, rituals and ethnic patterns. The universality of faith removes exclusive prefecture of theology, opening it up to a more diverse and holistic appreciation of spirituality and the personalized application of faith.

Third, faith involves ways of creating or constructing meaning that may or may not be religious in nature. Fowler (1981, 1986) contends that faith is two-dimensional: faith as a way of relating and faith as a way of knowing. Faith as knowing involves the process of making meaning that directs and speaks to one's orientation toward life. The knowing dimension of faith assists in making sense of our experiences.

Fourth, faith is interactive and social; it requires community, language, ritual, and nurture (Fowler, 1981). Functionally, Fowler (1981) asserts that individuals possess "centers' of value" and "images of power" which frame their beliefs, and constructs the "master stories" which guide their life (p. 276). According to Fowler (1981), all individuals have something in which or someone in whom they believe. There are acknowledged influential powers, life-directing narratives or myths of who they are, of who they should be, and of what life is all about. Regardless of whether this source of ultimate interest has a religious or a nonreligious application, it provides organizing principles of existence and a backdrop of shared meaning with others (Driedger, 1997; Fowler, 2004).

Fifth, faith encompasses ones response to the transcendent. While Fowler is not concerned with the individual identity of faith's "other", he is concerned with the content of one's faith (Fowler, 1981). The components of Fowler's definition of faith underscore his attention to the unique relational aspects of faith development in women as well as the structural characteristics of faith upon which his stage theory was developed.

Structural Characteristics of Faith

Fowler (1980; 1991) emphasizes that his theory is the result of an analysis of seven structural aspects or characteristics of faith development. An individual's ability to progress in and through the stages of faith development depends on maturation across seven structural-developmental components of faith development (Fowler, 1978; 2004). The seven structural components include:

1. *Form of Logic* (cognition) - based on Piaget's (1970) theory of cognitive development; describes distinctive patterns of reason an individual employs to support their beliefs and attitudes about the world around them (Moseley, Farvis, & Fowler, 1986).

2. *Form of World-Coherence* (cognition) – involves examination of the way an individual imagines and constructs a coherent and meaningful experience of the world.

3. *Role-Taking* (social perspective taking) - based on Selman's (1980) research on social perspective taking; involves one's ability to consider the perspective of others as well as form judgments about them. This can fluctuate from ego-focused to mutuality.

4. *Locus of Authority* (personal authorization) - the way an individual responds and evaluates the position and viewpoints of those in authority.

5. *Bonds of Social Awareness* (widening social inclusiveness) - the quality and extent of one's capacity for both a deepening and widening of the imaginative construction of the perspectives of others.

6. *Form of Moral Judgment* (moral reasoning) - based on Kohlberg's (1981) theory of moral development, outlines phases of moral development that pertain to the universal principle of justice.

7. *Symbolic Function* - a developmental account of the growing capacities in humans for shaping and responding imaginatively to symbols, narratives, and rituals that invite participation in the sacred and that touch the deepest dimensions of our relatedness to the Divine.

The integration of these seven structural components of faith development provides the framework for foundational components that make up Fowler's stage theory.

Fowler's Stage Theory

Fowler's theory of faith development consists of six faith stages or "styles" (plus a "pre-stage" in infancy). Fowler's stages of faith provide a model by which faith can be assessed (Driedger, 1997). The model for faith development is not linear rather it is a flexible spiral of interaction between the individual and society (Fowler, 1981, 2006). Structurally, each stage builds upon the previous (Driedger, 1997; Fowler 1981). The sequence of stages provides a description of the different ways in which individuals make meaning regardless of tradition or cultural context (Driedger, 1997). Fowler (1981) views the stages as graduated, sequential, and representing increased cognitive maturity and personalization of an individual's spiritual "identity".

Stages of Faith Development

Pre-Stage Undifferentiated Faith or Primal Faith (Birth to age three)

In the time before language and conceptual thought are possible, the infant forms a basic sense of trust, of being at home in the world. Right or good is what is pleasant or exciting, while wrong or bad is what is unpleasant or painful. Self is at the center of the infant's world; there is no ability on the part of the infant to put oneself in another's place.

During this pre-stage, the infant is forming what Fowler calls "pre-images" of God or the Holy, and of the kind of world in which he/she lives. All that comes later in terms of faith is built on this basis of trust or mistrust. Future religious experience will either confirm or reinforce this basic trust.

The strength of faith at this stage is the fund of basic trust. The danger in this stage is the failure develop a sense of mutuality with others, resulting either in an excessive narcissism or in isolation. Transition to Stage One begins with the convergence of thought and language and the availability of symbols in speech and ritual play.

Stage One: Intuitive/Projective Faith (Age three to age six or seven)

"Intuitive/Projective faith is the fantasy-filled, imitative phase in which the child can be powerfully and permanently influenced by examples, moods, actions and stories of the visible faith of primary related adults" (Fowler, 1981, p. 133). The child experiences the world as fluid and full of novelty. This stage is a changing, growing, dynamic faith marked by the rise of imagination. The child does not have the type of logic that questions fantasies or perceptions Fowler refers to the child's mind as inquisitive and religiously malleable during this stage. Fowler is struck by the number of times that interviews showed that images formed during this stage have powerful and long lasting effects both positive and negative on faith development.

The strength of this stage is the birth of imagination. The dangers lie in the possible restriction of imagination by criticism or from the possible exploitation of imagination in the reinforcement of moral or doctrinal expectations. The factor precipitating transition to the next stage is the emergence of concrete operational thinking and the ability to distinguish between what is real and what only seems real.

Individuals demonstrate a significant amount of dependency on parental and other authority figures. They tend to demonstrate nave cognitive egocentrism and lack perspective thinking abilities. These individuals emphasize imagination and stories as the mechanisms of understanding and expressing spiritual or religious beliefs (Fowler, 1981; Fowler & Dell, 2006; Ripley, et al., 2007).

Stage Two: Mythic Literal Faith (Age Seven to Eleven or Twelve)

Mystic/Literal Faith is "the stage in which the individual begins to take on stories, beliefs, and observations that symbolize belonging to his or her faith community" (Fowler, 1981, p. 149). The episodic nature of the previous stage gives way to a more linear structure of meaning. Story telling now becomes the major vehicle for the expression of meaning. There is a sense of literalness to this stage, so the child cannot step outside of the story to reflect on its meaning.

However, there is an increased capacity to step outside the individual's own experience to encounter another's reality. Reciprocal fairness is an important moral issue at this stage.

The strength of this stage is the expansion of the individual's narrative as a way of understanding life experiences. Its limitations lay in a potential literalness and an overinvestment in reciprocity, which results in perfectionism or in a sense of "badness" resulting from neglect or mistreatment from significant others. Movement into Stage Three is precipitated by deviations in stories, which lead to reflections upon their meanings. Individuals continue to rely heavily on the guidance of authority figures such as parents and teachers, particularly through the transmission of spiritual and religious stories. In this stage, individuals develop improved capabilities for simple perspective taking and meaning making. However, they lack the ability to understand their own and others' inferiority (internal workings), and they typically exhibit black-and-white thinking. Also, there is a strong belief in justice and reciprocity of the universe (Fowler, 1981).

Stage Three: Synthetic/Conventional Faith (Ages Twelve to Seventeen or Eighteen)

At this stage, one's world extends beyond self and family so that a number of spheres demand attention: family, school, peers, and possibly the religious community. It is a time when individuals are deeply concerned about forming a spiritual or religious identity that they attempt to integrate into every part of their life. They are concerned about feedback from significant people in their lives. In a sense, it is a conformist stage, and faith must provide a means of synthesizing values and input from diverse arenas. Individuals pull together various parts of faith and tend to conform to the majority. They are rewarded or punished for following rules laid down by authorities. Views at this stage are often stereotyped.

One of the hallmarks of this stage is the tendency to perceive God in interpersonal terms as friend, companion, and guide. There seems to be a hunger for a God who knows and confirms the identity that is being shaped. While this is a stage that individuals typically move into during adolescence, for many adults it becomes a permanent position. In other words, many adults are functioning on a faith developed in adolescence. Often at this stage, "a person has an ideology and a more or less consistent clustering of values and beliefs, but he or she has not objectified it for examination and in a sense is unaware of having it" (Fowler, 1981, p.173).

The strength of this stage is the forming of a "personal myth"- - the myth of the individual's own becoming in faith and identity. The dangers are twofold: (a) the expectations of others can become so internalized that autonomy is hindered and (b) interpersonal betrayals can result in despair. Movement into Stage Four can be caused by a number of experiences that lead to critical reflection on one's values and beliefs, such as clashes between valued authorities or the upheaval of leaving home.

Individuals strive to form a spiritual or religious identity and attempt to integrate it in every part of their life. They begin to attend to their own interiority and that of others, a developmental milestone that is accompanied by a dramatic new capacity for social perspective taking and mutual interpersonal perspective taking. They continue to be somewhat rigid and self-focused in their approach to spiritual issues, and their dependency broadens to include not just authority figures, but also in groups as well. Conformity is key during this stage, with individuals striving to conform to their community's definition of faith. At this stage individuals align with a certain perspective of belief. Self is constituted and sustained by its relationships and roles. Consequently, individuals in stage three are extremely attuned to their relational contexts. Their central yearning is inclusion, sometimes to the point of risking interpersonal fusion.

Stage Four: Individuative-Projective Faith (Ages Twenty to Thirties and Forties)

According to Fowler, transitioning from stage three to four "is particularly critical for it is in this transition that the late adolescent or adult must begin to assume responsibility for his or her own commitments, lifestyles, beliefs, and attitudes. In movement towards stage four the individual must address unavoidable tensions; individuality verses being defined by a group or group membership; subjectivity and the power of one's strongly felt unexamined feelings verses objectivity and the requirement of critical reflection; self-fulfillment or self-actualization as a primary concern verses service to and being there for others; the question of being committed to the relative versus struggle with the possibility of an absolute" (Fowler, 1981, p. 182). There is a relocation of authority within the self along with a critical reflection of one's beliefs. Faith becomes uniquely one's own.

Stage four takes form in young adulthood. However, for some, progression to this stage may be halted. This stage requires the development of a new self-identity and a new outlook or worldview that is now differentiated from the identities and outlooks of significant others. Symbols are now translated into conceptual meanings and institutional religion may be seen as too conventional.

The strength of stage four lies in the capacity for critical self-reflection. Its danger lies in the inability to establish a balance between the reflective nature of critical self-examination and naive self-confidence in the conscious mind and critical thought. Movement into the next stage (stage 5) is brought on by restlessness with the identity and meanings formed in stage four and recognition that one has compromised too. There is a realization of a broader meaning of life and individuate of spiritual belief. Individuals in stage four critically examine the system of beliefs, symbols, values and commitments they previously accepted uncritically. They develop a new social perspective-taking capacity while starting to take on a new authority in defining and directing them. Individuals in this stage commonly define themselves over and against other faith groups, often comparing systems of thought dichotomously. In this stage there is critical reflection of one's own beliefs. This stage is often filled with angst as the individual's faith becomes his or her own.

Stage Five: Conjunctive Faith (Rare before the later thirties)

Conjunctive Faith requires deeper self-reflection and involves a reworking of one's past. The individual is ready for a new kind of intimacy with those who are different. This involves "a critical recognition of one's social unconsciousness-the myths, ideal images and prejudices build deeply into the self-system by virtue of one's nurture within a particular social class, religious tradition, ethnic group or the like" (Fowler, 1981, p, 198).

Truth is now seen as many-sided and if it is to be grasped holistically individuals must see several sides at once. Contradictions are more easily tolerated and individuals are willing to be vulnerable to the truths of others. Individuals can appreciate symbols, myths and rituals (one's own and others) because they grasp the reality to which they refer.

The strength of this stage is the capacity to experience the power of the individual's or the group's symbols and meaning, while recognizing that they are only partial. Its danger lies in a sense of emotional complacency or withdrawal if overwhelmed by the paradoxes of reality. However, "…this stage remains divided. It lives and acts between an untransformed world and a transforming vision and loyalties. In some few cases this division yields to the call of the radical actualization that we call Stage 6" (Fowler, 1981, p.198).

Stage Six: Universalizing Faith

Reaching Stage 6 is "exceedingly rare". The persons best described by it have "generated faith compositions in which their felt sense of an ultimate environment is inclusive of all being. They have an internalized and personalized depth of inclusive and fulfilled human community (Fowler, 1981). These individuals exhibit qualities that challenge conventional criteria of religious normalcy.

These individuals are more intentional and simple, yet immensely liberating and even subversive in their liberating quality. Fowler (1982) suggests Martin Luther King Jr., Thomas Merton, Mother Teresa of Calcutta, Abraham Heschel and Gandhi are examples of individuals who exhibited characteristics associated with stage six. Their community is universal and they find community with individuals from other faith stage and other faith tradition (Cowden, 1992).

The faith development stages provide a framework for understanding how maturation of individualized faith is a function of time, experience, challenges/life crises, and relational nurture. Fowler (1981) maintains that the sequential nature of faith progression does not imply superiority of one stage over another. Nor are the stages intended to be a template for establishing therapeutic goals. Rather, Fowler's stages of faith development provide valuable insight into an individual's ability to internalize complex concepts in a manner that fosters intrinsic and extrinsic meaning-making and constructive interpretation of their relationships with others and the divine.

Fowler's Research

Fowler's (1981) theory is based on research reported in his book *Stages of Faith.* The results are based on structured interviews with 359 individuals, over a three-year period. Fowler's sample was evenly divided by gender and distributed throughout age categories 3 ½ to 84 years of age. However, it included a disproportionate number of Caucasians and those who identified their faith experience as Christian. Data were collected during a two to three hour open-ended semi-structured interviews. Because he did not wish to test the interviewee's definition of faith or religious beliefs, Fowler kept the purpose of the interview intrinsically focused. He introduced questions with religious nuances late in the interview. During the interview, respondents were asked to share aspects of their history and to express feelings and attitudes toward a variety of life issues that Fowler believed ones faith addressed. From the interviews, Fowler generated a set of existentially focused themes that corresponded with questions of faith or meaning making. These were: (a) death and afterlife; (b) the limits of knowledge; (c) causation and effect in personal and historical life; (d) evil and suffering; (e) freedom and determinism; (f) power and agency; (g) meaning of life; (h) ideal manhood or womanhood; (i) the future; (j) grounding of ethical and moral imperatives; (k) communal identifications and belonging; (l) bases of guilt and shame; (m) loyalties and commitments; (n) locus of transcendent beauty, value, or power; (o) objects of reverence or awe; (p) grounds of terror or dread; (q) sin and violation; (r) religious experiences, (s) religious beliefs and practices; and (t) specific meaningful religious symbols (Fowler & Vergote, 1981). The interviews were taped, transcribed, and analyzed based on the seven structural aspects or characteristics of a faith stage described previously. Interview questions were assigned to aspects/characteristics. Assigned measures/scores for questions assigned to a given aspect/characteristic were averaged and an overall score was given for each of the seven aspects. Finally, all aspect scores were averaged to yield a score from which stage assignment was made.

Updates to Fowler's Faith Development Theory Manual

The Stages of Faith Development theory has continued to evolve (Fowler et al., 2004). Its evolution reflects Fowler's foresight and commitment to the diverse application of the Spiritual

Development Model across gender and ethnicity. *Development of the Faith Development Instrument and Scoring Manual* (Moseley, et al., 1986) promoted standardization in administration and scoring instrumentation. Test for inter-rater reliability yielded agreement in the ninety percent range (Dykstra & Parks, 1986).

Fowler, Streib, and Keller (2004) developed the third and most recent edition of the *Manual for Faith Development Research.* The third edition advanced the work presented in preceding editions in several ways. First, it provides more systematic attention to the seven structural aspects or characteristics that taken together describe the structural aspects of a faith stage. Examination of each aspect enhances discrimination of the structural and content variations (or absences) in respondents' faith. Second, the introduction of computerized scoring improved the rapidity and accuracy of qualitative and quantitative analysis. Third, the *Faith Development Manual* and research instrument was translated into multiple languages. Fourth, revision of the manual allowed for the incorporation of the latest in cross-cultural research regarding faith development theory. This prompted the inclusion of an expanded bibliographic section that includes writings the authors feel contribute to a more advanced holistic perspective of the complexity and multidimensionality of faith from a lifespan perspective.

Theoretical and Empirical Evaluations of Faith Development Theory

Fowler's (1981) theory of faith development has attracted attention and inspired theoretical and empirical research in the United States and worldwide (Streib, 2005). To date over 53 empirical studies have used Fowler's faith development instrument or a variation thereof (Streib, 2005). Additionally, over one hundred dissertations were located for which Fowler's faith development theory constituted at least a significant position (Streib, 2003; Streib, 2005). Out of this number, approximately ninety dissertations focus primarily or exclusively on

Fowler's faith development theory (Streib, 2003; Streib, 2005). Eleven address the applicability of faith development within in religious education, pastoral care, and church work (Streib, 2003; Streib, 2005).

Critique of Fowler's Theory

Collections of four essays summarize insights of commentators and critics of faith development research and theory (Astley & Francis, 1992; Dystra & Parks, 1982, 1986; Fowler, 2004). Critiques of Fowler's theory of Faith address three consistent, yet differing themes. The first critique challenges the structural developmental aspects of faith development theories collectively. Fernhout (1986) questioned the construct and criterion validity of the stages of faith development. Specifically, Fernhout regarded faith development as essentially another way of evaluating moral development or worldview. The principal concern rests in the difficulty in defining faith in a functional and structural form that is inclusive of the dynamics of faith in many traditions and for some groups who hold secular ideologies. Likewise, Kohlberg (1981) criticized the lack of specificity in Fowler's (1982) definition of faith. Kohlberg maintained that Fowler's broad definition of faith did not distinguish it from moral judgment.

In contrast, Snarey (1991), in the most thoroughly published research to date, established the adequacy of the construct validity for faith development theory. He found strong evidence that the *Faith Development Interview* (Fowler, 1982) reflects a unified construct. All correlations between aspects were positive, moderately strong and highly significant. The alpha among the aspects was .93. In a factor analysis of aspect scores, there was only one factor with an eigenvalue greater than one. This factor accounted for 74% of the variance. Finally, 78% of research participants' aspect scores were within the range of one stage across all aspects. These findings support the construct validity of the *Faith Development Interview*.

With regard to criterion validity, Snarey (1991) found that faith development was related to, but not reducible to, moral development ($r = .60 < .001$) and ego development ($r = .43$, $p < .001$. Thus, faith development and moral development are separate constructs. Additionally, Snarey found that variables reflective of societal standing were effective in distinguishing levels of faith development. Faith development was related to education ($r = .49$, $p < .001$), occupation ($r = .45$, $p < .001$), social class ($r = .43$ $p < .001$), and work complexity ($r = .49$, $p < .001$). These relationships were maintained even after controlling for other developmental domains.

The second criticism addresses the sampling procedures of Fowler's (1981) research. Specifically, the commentators question the universality of Fowler's findings, noting that he did not work with a random sample and that some groups were over or under represented (Rich & DeVitis, 1985). Specifically noted were the lack of cross-cultural testing and a substantial dependency upon Judeo-Christian tradition. However, the range of overall faith development scores in Snarey's (1991) research with secular Kibbutzes gave evidence for the cross-cultural universal application of faith development theory to religious and nonreligious individuals.

The third theme addresses controversy regarding gender differences and skewed gender representation among faith development stages. Although Fowler's (1981) research, unlike that of Kohlberg (1981) involved subjects evenly divided by gender categories, various gender-specific studies maintain that Fowler's theory fails to recognize and emphasize inimitable developmental expressions of faith in women, particularly those of relational connectedness defined by care and responsibility over principles and rights (Cowden, 1992; Devor, 1989; Devor, 1989; Dykstra & Parks, 1986; Gilligan, 1982).

Carol Gilligan in her 1977 article and her 1982 book, *In a Different Voice* disputes the adequacy of Kohlberg (1982) and Fowler's (1981) hierarchical sequence in expressing and explaining poignant developmental gender differences with regard to moral and spiritual orientation. According to Gilligan (1982), there are two gender directed avenues of moral development and expression. One more representative of female development is based on expressions of empathy, care and relationships with others. Another, more characteristic of males is based on issues of justice, fairness, and individual rights (Sias, 2002). Gilligan hypothesized that females were biologically endowed with a moral orientation of care and men toward an orientation of justice. Given the established gender difference, Devor (1989) and Gilligan (1982) assert that Fowler's description of the relational aspects of faith development are based on a male-biased philosophical construct and therefore excludes the feminine experience. This is evident, according to Gilligan, in a gender weighted distribution of men and women among the stages of faith development. Specifically, issues reflective of care and concern are rated lower (Stage 3) than issues of justice (Stage 4 and higher). Limitations in the theoretical construct are, therefore, interpreted as weakness in women's developmental progress which suggests that women are less spiritually/morally mature (Gilligan, 1982). Fowler (2004) suggests that while these variations may suggest a relationship between age and gender and the stages of faith, further analysis on a larger more scientifically drawn sample is needed to evaluate whether the results were due to an uneven distribution of men and women across age groups or, as Gilligan suggests, the result of a gender-biased construct.

Investigating Gilligan's (1982) gender-stage differentiation hypothesis, Kerber (1986) Geeno and Maccoby (1986) and Luria (1986) challenged the methodology of Gilligan's research and expressed concerns regarding several of Gilligan's assumptions. Keber (1986) questioned Gilligan's assertion that women are biologically predisposed to an orientation to care. Regarding women as biologically predisposed to caring and relationships supports gender dichotomies and advance gender role stereotypes (Sias, 2002) Similarly, Kerber (1986) and Greeno and Maccoby (1986) suggested that the gender differences Gilligan described are more manifestations of socialization and culture rather than biological factors. Thus, issues of diversity in socialization and culture would be more accurate determinants of an individual's capacity for empathetic and altruistic responses.

In a methodological critique of Gilligan's (1982) research, several limitations were identified: problems with the sample size, ambiguously defined variable parameters (age, social class, education, and method of recruitment), generalizability and replicability of the findings, indistinct delineation between theoretical speculation and evidentiary data, limited information concerning a reliable scoring method, and the lack of an appropriate rationale for combining sources for data on gender and moral development (Donleavy, 2008; Luria, 1986). According to Luria, age, social class, education, and method of recruitment must carefully identify a credible sample so that readers can apply the findings to similar groups. Gilligan's sample of eight males and eight females of different ages is not representative of all males and females. Nor is the subsequent application of the stages of moral development equal to that of Fowler's stages of faith development (Snarey, 1991). Smetena (1984) questioned Gilligan's lack of clear guidelines for scoring and the use of hypothetical dilemmas. Smetena insisted that an adequate test of Gilligan's hypotheses would require a scoring system that looked for separate paths of development for men and women with standardization that would allow for the replication of her study. Similarly, Walker, Reed, O'Neil & Brown (2009) criticized Gilligan for using anecdotal data. Additionally, Kerber (1986) disputed Gillian's claim that women are biologically predisposed to an orientation of care. Kerber suggested that the differences Gillian described in men and women are due to socialization and culture. Due to these limitations, more research is needed in the area of women's spiritual formation.

Fowler's theory of faith development has provided a comprehensive lifespan perspective of religious and spiritual development (Cartwright, 2001). His contributions have been influential in advancing research regarding the interpersonal (intrinsic) and intrapersonal (extrinsic) role of faith, spirituality, and spiritual well-being in the areas of mental health and pastoral counseling, developmental psychology religious education (Cartwright, 2001; Parker, 2006).

Faith, Spirituality and Well-Being

Applied interchangeably throughout literature, spirituality and faith are definitionally complex concepts (Cashwell & Young, 2005; Miller & Thorensen, 2003; Pargament, 1997). Differentiation of disposition, scope, and integration of faith and spirituality provides valuable insight into their distinct yet inter-connected impact on spiritual development (Hey, Reicht, & Utsch, 2006). Thoresn and Harris (2002), and Miller and Thoresen (2003) define religious aspects of faith as a societal and institutional phenomenon. Although often encompassing elements of spirituality, religion is expressed through a set of beliefs and practices that involve social institutions composed of members who abide by various rituals, covenants, rules, and formal procedures. Spiritual aspects of faith encompass the individual's intrinsic and extrinsic search for and experience of the sacred (Hill & Pragament, 2003; Thoresen & Harris, 2002). Specific uses of the terms intrinsic and extrinsic have been refined. They are built upon the distinctions originally proposed by Allport & Ross (1967) Intrinsic spirituality encompasses characteristics of spirituality that are "the product of internalized controls" (Beck and Miller, 2000, p. 316). More specifically, intrinsic spirituality is motivated by spirituality is motivated by feelings of personal conviction and commitments rather than external rewards (Beck & Miller, 2000). Fowler referred to these as "centers of value" and Images of power" which frame beliefs and construct "master stories" which guide their lives (Fowler, 1981, p. 276). Extrinsic spirituality refers to beliefs or behaviors which are influenced by relationships with others, group expectations, or other external controls. Fowler (1981) identified interactive and social or intrinsic aspects of faith development (community, language, ritual and nurture) as necessary for spiritual development. This relational aspect of development is viewed as an essential aspect of faith/spiritual development in women (Astley, 2009; Belenky, 1989; Devor, 1989; Fowler, 1991; Gilligan, 1982). For the current study, intrinsic and extrinsic spirituality will be operationalized through the use of the Spiritual Well-Being Scale (Ellison, 1982).

While commonly connected to formal religious practices, spirituality is continuous and broad in dimension (Miller, 1999). Spiritual well-being provides a theoretical and definitional framework for merging intrinsic and extrinsic components of spirituality and faith in a manner that permits overarching assessment of spiritual wellness and spiritual development (Gill, Barrio-Minton, & Myers, 2010). Further, Westgate (1996) identified four themes, notably similar to those presented in Fowler's (1981) theory, considered essential for the promotion of spiritual wellness and well-being: (a) purpose and meaning in life, (b) fundamental life defining values, (c) transcendence, and (d) a community of shared values.

Spirituality and Mental Health

The contribution of religious and spiritual praxes to physical and psychological wellness and well-being is widely supported (Ellison & Levin, 1998; Ellison & Larson, 2002; Hill & Pargament, 2003; Hadzic, 2011; Seybold & Hill, 2001; Smith, McCullough & Poll, 2003; Thorensen, 1999). In a review of empirical studies, several authors support the mitigating elements of religious and spiritual practice in the promotion of: (a) greater life satisfaction, (b) posttraumatic growth, (c) positive coping strategies, (d) improved health outcomes, and (e) diminished levels of depression and depressive symptomatology (Johnson, Thompkins, & Webb, 2002; Khalsa, 2003; Pargament, Koenig, Tarakeshwar, & Hahn, 2004; Richards, 2000; Smith et al., 2000). Their findings were inclusive of diverse faith traditions as well as racial and ethnic groups in the United States.

Challenges to healthy psychological development for at risk youth prompted Davis, Kerr, and Robinson Kurpius (2003) to examine whether spiritual and religious variables augment adolescent psychological development. They evaluated the relationship between spirituality and anxiety in at-risk adolescents. Specifically, adolescents between the ages of 13 and 19 who (a) live in an impoverished economic setting, (b) exhibit poor academic performance, (c) display characteristics of low self-esteem, (d) exhibit a propensity for risk taking behaviors (e.g., unsafe sexual practices, substance abuse, delinquency) or (e) who are exposed to models for deviant behavior were included in the study. Four paper and pencil instruments: The *State-Trait Anxiety Inventory*, which differentiates between transitory (state) and characteristic (trait) anxiety, the *Spiritual Well-Being Scale*, which distinguishes between the religious and existential dimensions of spirituality, a revised version of the *Allport-Ross Religious Orientation Scale*, designed to measure both intrinsic and extrinsic religiosity and the *Social Provisions Scale,* a 24-item instrument measuring six social provisions, (a) attachment (caring), (b) social integration (belonging to a group of similar others) (c) reliable alliance (tangible assistance), (d) guidance (advise and information), (e) reassurance of worth (positive evaluation), and (f) opportunity for nurturance (support to others), were administered to 45, (25 females and 20 males) high school students from culturally and religiously diverse backgrounds. Results suggested that the higher the spiritual well-being among males, the lower the level of anxiety. However, only lower existential well-being was associated with lower anxiety among females. Caution in interpreting this study was noted as the sample cannot be considered representative of all at-risk adolescents; therefore results cannot be generalized to the general population. Additionally, their preliminary analyses revealed that female participant scores yielded more elevated trait anxiety scores than male participants. Higher trait anxiety scores among female participants may be attributed to three factors. First, gender differences exist in patters of male and female socialization. Scores on existential well-being may reinforce the importance of relational aspects of well-being in women. Second, young women encounter more barriers to personal, professional, and financial achievement than young men, including training, prejudicial treatment in school, discrimination in the workplace and lack of resources. These barriers, particularly prejudicial and discriminatory treatment, are often more imposing for young women of color, who composed over half of the female sample in this study. Third, female participants may experience a diminished sense of self-esteem that may result in increased levels of anxiety.

Enlow, Blood, and Egeland (2013) assert that children under the age of six have been largely excluded from traumatic stress studies. However, evidence suggests that young children under the age of six years are at elevated risk for exposure to maltreatment, and may be highly vulnerable to severe and persistent traumatic stress responses and other negative developmental sequelae (Briggs-Gowan, Carter and Ford, 2012; Center for Disease Control and Prevention, 2010).

Enlow et al. (2013) examined associations between co-occurring interpersonal trauma exposure. Specifically, maltreatment (evidence of any physical abuse, emotional abuse including constant harassment or berating, chronically finding fault, harsh criticism, emotional neglect including emotional unresponsiveness, physical neglect or sexual abuse, defined as genital contact between the child and a person at least 5 years or older) and witnessing interpersonal violence (frequency and severity of physical violence toward the mother by her partner in the home as reposted by the mother) on developmental competence, and childhood PTSD symptoms in a community of low-income birth cohort followed to first grade. The study contained 200 dyads (mother and child). The racial and ethnic composition of the children was 65% Caucasian, 18% multiracial, 12% Black, 4% Native American, 1 % Hispanic and, 5% Asian. 45% of the children were female. Participants completed multiple interviews including in-home and clinical test center observations between the child's birth and age 7 years. Maternal interviews were conducted around the time of he child's birth and at 12, 18, 24, 30, 42,48, 54, and 64 months and when the children were in the first grade. The findings revealed that between birth and 64 months of age, 38% of participants witnessed interpersonal trauma with 28% experiencing maltreatment. Among those experiencing maltreatment, 49% were physically abused, 54% emotionally maltreated, 48% neglected and 18% were sexually abused. Exposure to any interpersonal trauma was associated with greater lower school age competence and a higher incidence of childhood traumatic stress symptoms. Further, Enlow et al., (2013) contend that traumatic episodes involving the caregiver as perpetrator or victim appear especially damaging to a child's mental health and early developmental processes. While developmental processes were explored, spiritual development was not included as part of the study.

Briggs-Gowan, Carter, and Ford (2012) and Masters and Curtis, (2000) substantiate the harm of childhood traumatic stress symptoms on adolescent and adult emotional and behavioral development. They suggest that prior forms of adaptation become hierarchically integrated into later patterns of behavioral and emotional adaptations that interfere with developmental milestones and the ability to use internal and external resources to successfully negotiate developmentally salient issues. Thus, victims of violence and maltreatment can become perpetrators of violence and maltreatment.

It is often in the context of counseling that clients begin to explore issues of spirituality, recognizing religious and spiritual queries as part of individual faith development invites examination of intrinsic and extrinsic purpose and meaning during times of increased stress, health crisis, and traumatic events (Gall & Grant, 2005; Haynes, 2009; Holcomb & Nonneman, 2004). The inclusion of spiritual dimensions within the delivery of counseling services contributed to improved treatment compliance and enriched long-term recovery efforts (Atenn & Hernandez, 2004; Miller, 2003; St. Hillaire, 2010).

Davis, Kerr, and Robinson Kurpius' (2003) findings are consistent with Fowler's (1984) research regarding the dissonance experienced as adolescents and young adults transition from stage two, *Mystic-Literal Faith* to stage three, *Synthetic-Conventional Faith.* Common to adolescence, transition to stage three represents a turning point in faith development. Cognitive capacity expands and allows the introduction of logical and hypothetical thinking (Piper, 2004). However, difficulty applying the capacity for critical thinking to their personal faith stems from the tendency to hold faith values of parents, peers and faith groups, while questioning the validity of those values (Fowler, 1981; 1995).

Recognition of spirituality as a fundamental yet diverse aspect of culture has led to the development of professional organizations focusing on the inclusion of individual spiritual beliefs in counseling. In fact, the training bodies of several organizations (American Psychological Association [APA]; American Counseling Association [ACA]; Counsel for Accreditation of Counseling and Related Educational Programs, [CACREP]) have specific curriculum requirements in the area of spirituality (Miller 2003; Stebnicki, 2006; St. Hillaire, 2010).

Faith as a foundational component in the provision of comprehensive holistic care is not only well documented (Cashwell, Myers & Shurts, 2004; Courtenay, Merriam & Reeves, 1999; Hee, 2007; Mackinely, 2005; Merriam, 2007; and Parker, 2006), but it also reinforces the multidimensional application of *Faith Development Theory*. Holistic care supports the integration self-awareness, community support, and incorporation of the sacred.

Spirituality and Substance Abuse

The efficacy of spirituality in the treatment and recovery of addictive disorders is now widely recognized (Ciarrocchi & Brelsford, 2009; Galanter, Dermatis, Blunt, Williams, Trujillo, & Steinke, 2007; Juhnke, et al., 2009), based in part on the pioneering work of Alcoholics Anonymous (AA), a 12-step mutual support recovery group established in 1935 (Galanter et. al., 2007; Miller, 2002; Miller, 2003). The 12-step model endorses recovery as "a spiritual program" (Miller & Kurtz, 1994), which includes belief in a transcendental being or "higher power" outside of and greater than oneself. Although the nature of the higher power or God is intentionally broadly defined in the core literature of AA, the higher power is viewed as a personal and active source of help and hope for those seeking to recover (Miller, 2002). The successes experienced as a result of the beliefs and practices of AA have contributed to the development of other 12-step, spiritual recovery programs such as Narcotics Anonymous and Alanon (Miller, 2002). In fact, many of the approaches now used in addiction treatment are based on a 12-step model known as the "Minnesota model", which integrates counseling strategies with the spiritual principals of Alcoholics Anonymous (Miller, 2002).

White, Wampler and Fischer (2001) operationalized and measured levels of spirituality among 183 males and 69 females from a variety of 12-step, medical model treatment settings. Three measures, the *Spiritual Health Inventory* (internal and external spiritual well-being; Chappell, 1995), the *Surrender Scale* (Reinert et al., 1995) and the *Life Orientation Test* (a measure of optimism; Scheier & Carver, 1985) were utilized to determine whether elevated levels of spirituality were associated with measures of successful recovery (longer lengths of abstinence, more integrated recovery behaviors, and perceived quality of recovery). Results suggested that integration of spiritual practices are predictive of measures of successful recovery as well as the quality of recovery, mastery of twelve-step constructs, principals of surrender, and intrinsic levels of spiritual well-being. External spiritual well-being was negatively correlated with years of education but positively correlated with age. In general, measures of spirituality successfully differentiated between recovery lengths, recovery behaviors, and perceived quality of recovery. Additionally, individuals who had achieved one or more years of sobriety were found to have higher levels of internal spirituality, well-being, and optimism scores than those with less than one year of sobriety. They did not find gender differences with regard to the levels of spirituality.

White, Wampler and Fischer (2001) findings bolster Fowler's (1984) theoretical belief that spiritual development (evident in stages three through five) influence the individual's ability to internalize complex ideas and perspectives such as surrender, powerlessness, unmanageability and higher power (12-step constructs). Likewise, spiritual development foster's internal meaning-making and connection to members of a shared community (attendance of 12-step meetings).

Spirituality and Trauma

The impact of trauma is multifaceted, evidenced and expressed physically, cognitively, behaviorally, psychologically, sociologically and spiritually. Trauma confounds prevailing religious and spiritual constructs and necessitates reorganization and reconstruction of spiritual assumptions, internal value system, worldview, and sense of meaning (Shaw, Joseph & Linley, 2005; Vis & Boynton, 2008).

Smith (2006) maintains that as individuals recover from trauma, spirituality and trauma become propitiously reciprocal. That is, traumatic event(s) impact the individual's spiritual development/integration, and spiritual orientation influences the individual's reaction to, and recovery from, the trauma experience. Thus, spiritual methods of coping can either promote progressive trauma interpretations that reinforce the recovery process or signal levels of spiritual distress that hinder treatment engagement and participation.

Just as there are critical periods in the development of many human attributes, the initial structures of meaning, personal value, and purpose are most efficiently and effectively established in early childhood (Garbarino & Bedard, 1996). Garbarino & Bedard, (1996) and Fowler (1981) suggest that there is a developmental framework for experiencing a sense of meaning and purpose for life. Trauma challenges the construction of this sense of meaning and purpose. The enormity of this challenge is greatest for childhood victims because they have under-developed cognitive skills necessary to making sense of the world, and they have not had the time to build a solid framework of meaning. Often, children are more open to concepts of spiritually than are adults in the sense that their experience of reality is less constricted by social conventions regarding what is real and what is not (Garbarino & Bedard, 1996). Magical thinking is an important feature of early childhood. It forms the basis for fantasy play, which itself is an important resource for children in developing and working through alternative scenarios as solutions for day to day issues and problems in their lives. Imagery of a higher power often includes a sense of a benevolent and protective ideal parent figure (Garbarino & Bedard, 1996). Trauma, both inflicted by, and inflicted upon another, can temporarily or permanently shatter spiritual assumptions and belief in a higher all-benevolent power (Garbarino & Bedard, 1996). These shattered assumptions can sever the intrinsic and extrinsic connection between the child's understanding of themselves as spiritual beings and the higher power they believe exists to protect them (Garbarino & Bedard, 1996).

Shaw, et al., (2005) conducted a systematic review of eleven empirical studies (four qualitative and seven quantitative) that identified links between religion, spirituality and posttraumatic growth. Three main findings were reported. First, religion and spirituality are beneficial in dealing with the aftermath of trauma. Second, traumatic experiences can lead to a deepening of one's religious or spiritual connection. Third, positive religious coping allows an openness and readiness to face existential questions, religious participation, and a deepening religious understanding. Shaw and colleagues identified each finding as necessary components for posttraumatic growth.

In a large study of women veterans, Chang, Skinner, and Boehmer (2001) surveyed 3,543 women who were a part of the Veterans' Administration (VA) Women's Health Project to explore the effect of religion on women veterans who had experienced sexual assault. This study emanated from growing attention to the frequency of sexual assault among women in the military. Thus, researchers were interested in sexual assault occurring in the military, as opposed to assault by a family member. In addition, the researchers were expressly interested in depression related to sexual assault(s). Of the women in Chang et al.'s (2001) sample, over half were in the Army, followed by 24% in the Air Force, 21% in the Navy, and 6% in the Marines. Most of the women were enlisted for 3 years or less, and approximately half of the women rated their military experience as positive. Out of the total sample, 804 women reported a sexual assault while in the military. The researchers compared the women who were sexually assaulted with a group of women who reported no sexual assault. They measured general mental health, level of depression, religious attendance, and subjective religious experience. The two groups of women were similar in age, ethnicity and religious attendance (i.e., likelihood to find their religion a source of strength). The researchers found the women who had been sexually assaulted reported increased levels of mental health difficulties (e.g., depression) and scored an average of seven points lower on the measure of general mental health. Between the two groups of participants, the women were likely to have higher mental health scores and lower depression scores when they reported integrated religious practice as a source of strength regardless of sexual assault history. Within the group of women who had been sexually assaulted, those who attended religious services regularly and found their beliefs comforting reported less mental distress and had lower scores in the measure of depression than those who did not practice their religion. The researchers concluded that religious practices have a "buffering" (p. 91) effect against the stress incurred by military sexual assault.

According to Chang et al. (2001), there were several limitations to their study. First, they note that the larger study is cross-sectional and observational. Therefore, confounding variables may influence results (i.e., high mental health scores may mean that the individual is more likely to practice religion). Secondly, the survey was only given to women who use the VA's services; and the researchers report that a small percentage of veterans actually go to VAs to receive their healthcare services. Furthermore, the researchers only used two questions to measure religiosity;

one question assessed amount of religious attendance, and the other was a yes or no question regarding religion as a source of strength.

Despite the limitations noted, the mitigating factors of integrated spiritual and religious practices on levels of depression were identified. From a faith development perspective, one's ability to engage in critical reflection of the sexual assault allows for the intrinsic and extrinsic meaning making, as well as reconstruction of a more individualized world view and integrated faith practices which, suggests cognitive progression and transition from stage three (Synthetic-Conventional Faith) to stage four (Individuative-Reflective faith) of Faith Development theory (Piper, 2004).

Like Chang et al. (2001), Kennedy, Davis, and Taylor, (1998) were interested in sexual assault perpetrated by someone outside the woman's family and who was not an intimate partner. The researchers studied the effect of sexual assault on women's spirituality and wellbeing. The researchers noted that ample research has explored specific traumatic events such as accidents and illness and spirituality. However, they argued that accidents and illnesses differ greatly from crime victimization, in that crime is an intentional harmful act perpetrated onto an innocent person. Kennedy et al. hoped to answer two questions: (a) To what extent do victims of sexual assault report a changed role in their understanding and expression of spirituality after the assault and (b) To what extent is a change in one's spiritual understanding related to change in overall well-being or recovery.

Kennedy et al. (1998) quantitatively studied 70 women who had been sexually assaulted by someone other than an intimate partner. The participants' age range was from 19 to 46, and the majority of the sample was African American. Most of the women had either a high school education or had some post-high school education, and most were of a lower socioeconomic status. Only 12% reported having no religious affiliation, while the largest affiliation was Baptist at 36%. The researchers measured well-being, spirituality, intrinsic religiosity, and severity of assault. Over half of the women reported that during the 9 to 24 months following the assault, the role of spirituality in their lives increased. Only 20% of the women reported that the role of spirituality decreased and the remaining 20% reported no change. Thus, the role of spirituality increased ($p < .0001$) for the assault victims. Of the African American women, 71% reported that the role of spirituality increased, compared to 54% of Latina women and 38% of Caucasian women. The research shows the importance of religion in the lives of women who are ethnic minorities. The researchers also found a positive correlation ($r = .54$, $p < .0001$) between women who reported increased spirituality and women who reported a higher sense of well-being. Likewise, women who reported that spirituality decreased were more likely to report a reduction in their well-being. Furthermore, the researchers found a correlation ($r = .67$, $p < .0001$) between intrinsic religiosity and an increase in spirituality. Kennedy et al.'s findings support the idea of posttraumatic growth, that is, the researchers found that the women experienced positive change through an increase in spirituality and an increase in well-being after the trauma experiences.

Kennedy et al (1998) noted several methodological limitations in their study. First, researchers of trauma are ethically prohibited in conducting randomized experiments. Further, there was not a without traumatized group with which to compare well-being and spirituality. Descriptive statistics are difficult to generalize; therefore, replicating the study with a control group would improve the methodology. The researchers suggested that spirituality and well-being after trauma be studied longitudinally in the future, which would also improve the methodology.

Cole, Benore, and Pargament (2004) and Falsetti, Resich, and Davis, (2003) contend that conservational (assimilative) and transformational (accommodative) spiritual frameworks provide effective coping strategies when facing difficult life circumstances and trauma. They suggest several religious coping methods as positive orienting strategies addressing the aftermath of traumatic experiences. First, spirituality helps individuals examine the implications and meaning the event has for their life and in their view of the world. These include interpretations of the trauma as teaching a spiritual lesson (benevolent reappraisals); seeking forgiveness from God as well as letting go of anger toward others; spiritual seeking of God's love and care; and viewing God as a friend or collaborator in facing the reality of trauma.

Second, inclusion of spirituality assists individuals in making sense of the experience (why it happened, who-if anyone-is to be held responsible). Third, spirituality cultivates relationship with others through formal and informal support offered in religious and non-religious spiritual communities. Similarly, these communities offer supportive avenues for individuals to talk about and redefine the experience in ways that are more manageable. Herman's (1992) work further supports the importance of restoring the connection between survivors and a supportive community. This connection allows for the re-construction of the trauma story in a manner that establishes a sense of internal and external safety.

Fourth, the integration of spirituality in trauma recovery allows individuals to identify and include spiritual and religious rituals as part of self-care. These spiritual practices can create a sense of internal awareness, calm, and safety while generating a sense of manageability of emotions (Vis & Boynton, 2008).

The above findings support Fowler's (1981) theory that faith development is fostered through ongoing informal and formal interactions with others in a shared community. It is in the context of community that the individual is able to develop a benevolent interaction with the divine, and construct meaning from the traumatic experience. This in turn prompts the development of an individual spiritual identity found in stages 3 through 5 of the *Spiritual Development Model.*

Similarly, Harrison, Koenig, Hays, Eme-Akward and Pargament, (2001) in a review of the literature on trauma and coping identify four characteristics of trauma progressing coping. These include spiritual connectedness, a collaborative partnership with God, benevolent reframing of the stressful or traumatic event, and seeking spiritual supports. Gall, Basque, Damasceno-Scott, and Vardy (2007) found that a survivor's perception about God as a benevolent rather than as a controlling figure was associated with lower rates of depression. They suggest the development and integration of a benevolent view of God offers a form of stable support and secure attachment. Additionally, they report that having a strong personal spirituality, but not necessarily a formal religious affiliation can serve as a coping resource in dealing with childhood sexual abuse.

Conversely, trauma researchers, recognize that a spiritual crisis often accompanies experiences of personal violation (Fallot, 1997; Herman, 1992; Janoff-Bulman, 1992; McCann & Pearlman, 1990). Experiences of trauma can adversely influence the individual's intrinsic and extrinsic spiritual experience and sense of spiritual well-being (Falsetti, Resick & Davis,). Cole (2004) and Harrison, et al., (2001) identify religious coping methods that signal spiritual distress or discontent. These include: feeling abandoned by God; a sense of being punished because of past sin or lack of devotion; and interpersonal spiritual discontent, defined as conflicts with one's religious community. Negative religious experiences have been identified as salient by feminist theologians working with trauma survivors (Brock & Parker, 2001; Fortune, 1991; Neuger,

2001). For instance, some women experience their religious traditions as minimizing or denying their experience (Nason-Clark, 1997). Practitioners and researchers report that religious communities often promote single theological solutions to deal with violence and abuse, such as unconditional forgiveness of the perpetrator; victims' accepting blame as punishment for sin, or concomitantly; and the importance of bearing suffering as increasing one's heavenly reward (Fortune, 1988, 2001; Nason-Clark, 1997). For survivors adverse theological beliefs or negative images of God often impede recovery (Fallot & Heckman, 2005). It may be more accurate to think of these cognitive processes as experiences of spiritual distress rather than as failures in religious and/or spiritual coping. Likewise, Fowler (1981) identified the ability to differentiate from negative theoretical or spiritual beliefs that accompany a life crisis often impede or delay progress in spiritual development and arrests movement in the faith stages.

Trauma and Substance Abuse

Substance abuse and trauma symptomology are the most common diagnoses to co-occur. Yet, trauma and addiction are perhaps the two most undiagnosed and misdiagnosed conditions counseling practitioners face (Davidson, 2001; Morgan, 2009; Najavitis, 2004). Trauma experiences are often at the core of co-occurring substance abuse and mental health issues (Kauffman, & Dore, 1995, Tuchman, 2010). Many women report the initiation of substance use subsequent to a specific traumatic event in their lives (Tuchman, 2010; Zlupko, Kauffman, & Dore, 1995). Among women in substance abuse treatment, fifty-five to ninety-nine percent report a history of trauma (Covington, Burke, Keaton, & Norcutt, 2008; Najavits, et al., 1997). Among women diagnosed with PTSD, 28% are estimated to develop an alcohol use disorder and 27% develop a drug use disorder (Najavitis, 1997; Morgan, 2009). Higher rates of comorbidity have been documented in clinical settings and among those with particular lifestyle vulnerabilities, such as veterans, prisoners, victims of domestic violence, and first responders (police, and firemen) (Najavits, 2007). Overall, those who are diagnosed as having posttraumatic stress disorder have three to four times greater risk for developing substance use disorders than those without a diagnosis (Morgan, 2009).

Fallott and Heckman (2005) examined the relationship between spirituality, well-being, and the effect of trauma on women co-diagnosed with a mental health disorder and a substance use disorder. The researchers used data collected in a previous survey funded by SAMHSA in Washington, DC and Stockton, CA to examine positive and negative styles of religious and/or spiritual coping in women who struggled with trauma and substance use. Fallot and Heckman's sample consisted of 666 female participants who were at least 18 years of age, diagnosed with an Axis I or Axis II mental disorder or a substance use disorder, and had a history of physical or sexual abuse. Demographically, approximately half of the women had not completed high school, and less than 20% were employed. Approximately half of the women received food stamps, and 75% had experienced homelessness at some point in their life. The majority of the Washington, DC sample was African-American, while the majority of the California sample was Caucasian. The researchers measured the religious coping, psychiatric symptoms, alcohol and drug use, and trauma history of their participants. The researchers found religious/spiritual coping was important in the lives of the women (Fallot & Heckman, 2005). Interestingly, when the researchers compared the women in their sample to women in the general population, they found both higher positive and higher negative coping in the women who had experienced trauma and substance use. After comparing the group from Stockton, CA with the group from Washington, DC, they found the women from Stockton reported more positive religious coping ($p < .001$), and the women from Washington, DC reported more negative religious coping ($p < .01$). They further compared ethnicity in the combined sample and found no significant difference between positive and negative religious coping. Thus, there were differences based on region of the United States but not ethnicity. Fallott and Heckman's (2005) findings suggested that severity of post-traumatic symptoms and other mental health symptoms were significantly related to spiritual coping styles. Fallot and Heckman (2005) found higher incidents of positive coping than negative coping, and they suggested that most of the women experience spirituality as a source of support rather than a source of conflict. There were fewer women who experienced spirituality or religion as a source of punishment or abandonment. More specifically, those with a benevolent view of God reported diminished post-traumatic and mental health symptoms. While those with more deleterious religious coping styles (view trauma/negative experiences as divine punishment or abandonment), reported exacerbations in the intensity and frequency of post-traumatic and mental health symptoms. This was particularly true for women who had experienced sexual abuse in childhood (as opposed to adulthood) ($p < .05$) or those who had experienced multiple traumas. In addition, Fallot and Heckman (2005) found religious coping was related to the severity of psychiatric symptoms. That is, women who experienced more intense symptoms also were more likely to report negative religious coping, while women who relied strongly on their religion or spirituality were more likely to have milder symptoms. The researchers also found higher spiritual coping and milder symptoms among African-American women, suggesting a cultural relationship as well. The researchers did not find a significant relationship between religious/spiritual coping and recovery from substance abuse.

Fallot and Heckman (2005) emphasized that future research consist of longitudinal studies to explore the relationship between severity of trauma and negative religious coping and the unexpected non-relationship between religious coping and substance abuse. They also suggested both positive and negative religious coping be considered when working with women who have experienced co-occurring trauma and substance use, and they stressed the necessity for mental health workers to give attention to the spirituality of their clients. The researchers discussed the clinical implications and future directions of their research at length but did not extensively discuss the limitations of their research. The primary limitation noted by this reviewer is that a large number of the participants were African American, and recent research indicates that they are more likely to use religious resources. This may have influenced the results of Fallot and Heckman's study.

Trauma Treatment

Comprehensive, gender-specific, trauma-inclusive evaluation is essential for holistic integration of healthcare services for women (Covington, 2008; Cusack, Frueh & Brady, 2007; SAMHSA, 2007). Few studies have evaluated potential traumatic event assessment instruments and their impact on trauma diagnosis and treatment (Najavitis, et al., 1998). Recent studies show that behaviorally-specific, comprehensive multiple-item tramatic event measures, such as the Traumatic Life Events Questionnaire (TLEQ; Kubany et al., 2000) provide more informative results than that of a single-question traumatic event assessment as reflected in the Structured Clinical Interview for DSM IV(SCID; First, et al. 1998). Comprehensive multiple traumatic event identification is critical to effective trauma diagnosis and treatment planning particularly among women (Cusack, Falsetti & De Arellano, 2002; Elhai, et al., 2005; Najavitis, et al., 1998).

In the transition from DSM III-R to DSM IV, the range of potential traumatic events was expanded to include indirectly experienced events; this resulted in a 59% increase in the prevalence of PTSD diagnosis. The increase in traumatic event identification due to DSM-IV criteria changes was attributed primarily to increased detection of traumatic events in women (Breslau & Kessler, 2001). Franklin, et al. (2002) and Elhai, et al. (2008) identified an increase in individual endorsement of traumatic event exposure with a multiple-item assessment verses the single item SCID assessment. However, neither Franklin et al. (2002) nor Elhai et al. (2008) concluded that the increased endorsement of traumatic events resulted in a significant overall increase in PTSD diagnosis. This supports previously reported research noted in Chapter 1 that only thirty-three to fifty-nine percent of women who identify a history of trauma occurrences meet diagnostic criteria for PTSD (Najavitis, et al., 1997). Often however, systemic and programmatic ideologies endorse single-focused, gender-neutral interventions that prohibit detection and treatment of the complex, often confounding needs of women who are impacted by trauma, mental illness, and substance abuse disorders (Covington, 2008; Cusack, et al., 2007; SAMHSA, 2007).

In recent years, critical advancements in the treatment of complex co-occurring disorders have occurred. These advancements include the promotion of integrated, gender-responsive, evidence-based *trauma-specific* and *trauma informed* treatment service models (Covington, et al., 2008; Elliot, Bjelajac, Fallot, Markoff & Reed, 2005; Najavits & Kanukollu, 2005; SAMHSA, 2007). Trauma-informed services refer to the education of staff regarding trauma and posttraumatic stress disorder. Trauma-specific services refer to the integration of therapy models or interventions that directly address trauma and posttraumatic stress disorder (Najavits & Kanukollu, 2005).

Gender-Responsive Services

Addiction treatment services for women based on a holistic woman-centered approach acknowledges an understanding of the distinguishing life experiences of women including the prevalence of traumatic events and the impact those events have on treatment presentation, symptomology, retention, and completion (Covington, et al., 2008). Owen and Covington (2003) conducted a multidisciplinary review of research related to a women's experience of substance abuse, trauma, health education, mental health, and employment. Their findings contributed to the development of foundational guidelines for effective treatment of women. These guidelines include: (a) recognition of gender differences; (b) therapeutic environment needs to be based on safety, respect, and dignity; (c) organizational policies, practices and programming need be relationally focused and promote healthy connections to children, family, significant others, and the community; and (d) service provision needs to address substance abuse, trauma, and mental health in a comprehensive, integrative, and culturally relevant manner.

Trauma-Informed Services

As the understanding of traumatic experiences in the lives of women increases, service providers must be proactive and intentional in understanding the conceptual framework of trauma theory and its applicability to clinical practice (Covington, et al., 2008). This includes organizational commitment and operational execution of a trauma–informed and trauma-focused service practices. (Elliott, et al., 2005).

Building on the foundational work of Harris and Fallot (2001) which examined organizational components of trauma-informed and trauma specific service practices, Elliott et al., (2005) examined ways to join practice (service delivery) and philosophy (trauma theory, empowerment theory and relational theory). Specifically, their work identifies and operationalizes ten principles that define trauma informed services in eight different gender specific service areas. These areas include: (a) recognize the impact of violence and victimization on development and coping strategies; (b) identify recovery from trauma as a primary goal; (c) employ an empowerment model; (d) strive to maximize a woman's choices and control over her recovery; (e) are based in a relational collaboration; (f) create an atmosphere that is respectful of survivors' need for safety, respect and acceptance; (g) emphasize a woman's strengths, and highlight adaptations over symptoms and resilience over pathology; (h) minimize the possibilities of re-traumatization; (i) strive to be culturally competent and to understand each woman in the context of her life experiences and cultural background; and (j) solicit consumer input and involve consumers in designing and evaluating services.

Trauma-Specific Services

Cocozza, Jackson, Hennigan, Morrissey, Reed, Fallot, and Banks, (2005) and Morrissey, et al., (2005) utilized data from the Women Co-Occurring Disorders and Violence Study (WCDVS) to evaluate the efficacy of integrated trauma-informed and trauma-specific service provision at administrative and programmatic levels. Cocozza et al. (2005) evaluated six-month follow-up outcome data. Morrissey, et al., (2005) evaluated twelve-month follow-up outcome data.

The goal of the WCDVS study was to develop and test the effectiveness of service approaches specifically designed for women with frequent treatment utilization who presented with co-occurring disorders (Morrissey et al., 2005). The nine-site quasi-experimental, intent-to-treat outcome study was conducted from 2001 to 2003. In accordance with the SAMHSA federal guidelines, intervention groups were required to incorporate six core elements: resource coordination, crisis intervention, trauma-informed staff, holistic treatment of mental health, trauma, and substance abuse issues including behavioral, emotional, cognitive, and interpersonal consequences of trauma, trauma-specific service interventions, and involvement of participants in service planning and provision. SAMHSA did not stipulate a specific treatment model or trauma specific intervention. Conceptually similar, this flexibility allowed variability in the type of treatment setting. For example, in some sites, services were provided primarily on an outpatient basis while in others, they occurred in a residential setting; some interventions were provided in a setting that was primarily a substance abuse agency, others in a mental health agency environment. Similarly, variation existed in the provision of trauma-specific intervention. Four different manual-driven trauma-specific curriculums were implemented. One site used the *Addiction and Trauma Recovery Integration Model* (Miller & Guidry, 2001); four used the *Seeking Safety Model* (Najavitis, 2002); three used the *Trauma Recovery and Empowerment Model* (TREM) (Harris, 1998); and one developed a hybrid model called *Triad* (Clark & Fearday, 2001). Likewise, comparison conditions were not uniform. General guidelines provided by SAMHSA helped to ensure that comparisons were selected in the same geographical area and served similar women. Nonetheless, the characteristics of the comparison conditions varied widely, in length of and elements of usual care.

Instrumentation across the nine sites was uniform. Substance use problem severity, mental health symptoms, and trauma symptoms were measured in interviews with participants at baseline, six months, and 12 months. Problem severity of drug and alcohol use was assessed with the *Addiction Severity Index* (ASI) (McClellan, Luborsky, O'Brien & Wood, 1980). The drug composite score (ASI-D) and the alcohol composite score (ASI-A) measured problem severity during the past 30 days. Possible scores range from 0 to 1, with higher scores indicating greater problem severity of substance use. The ASI-A score was modified slightly in consultation with the author of the ASI, but it was scored on the original scale. Mental health symptoms were assessed with the *Global Severity Index* (GSI) of the *Brief Symptom Inventory* (Derogatis, 1993). The *Brief Symptom Inventory* is a 53-item self-report scale that measures nine symptom dimensions. Respondents are asked how much a problem has distressed them in the past seven days. Possible responses range from 0, not at all, to 4, extremely. The GSI is a mean severity measure. Possible scores range from 0 to 4, with higher scores indicating more severe symptoms. Trauma symptoms were assessed with the *Posttraumatic Symptom Scale* (PSS) of the *Posttraumatic Diagnostic Scale* (PDS, Foa, Cashman, Jaycox et al., 1997). The 17-item PSS was developed to assess the severity of trauma symptoms. Respondents were asked to indicate how often in the past month they have experienced a list of problems after a traumatic event. Possible responses range from 0, not at all or almost always. Possible scores range from 0 to 51, with higher scores indicating more severe trauma symptoms.

Eligible study participants were recruited independently at each location from a pool of women who had recently been referred for services. A total of 2026 women had data at the 6 and12-month follow-up: 1018 in the intervention group and 1,008 in the treatment as usual intervention. Women represented diverse racial and ethnic backgrounds: 17% were Hispanic; 50%, were White non-Hispanic; 25% were Black non-Hispanic; 7% were other non-Hispanic. One third of the sample was married or partnered. Most (70%) had experienced homelessness; half (51%) reported a current serious physical illness or disability.

Cocozza et al.'s (2005) six-month outcome comparison of program level effects indicated significant improvement in posttraumatic symptomology ($p < 0.02$), severity of substance use ($p < 0.02$), and mental health symptoms ($p < 0.06$) in the integrated trauma-informed/trauma-specific treatment models. The effect of the intervention is not consistent across sites. In fact, there is considerable variation across the nine participating sites. Thus, although as a whole the intervention sites displayed better outcomes, there was a significant amount of heterogeneity among sites. In some, women in the intervention conditions clearly did better than those in the comparison groups but in other cases there was little difference and in some cases women in usual care actually did better. This variability is consistent with the manner in which the intervention services were developed.

The final question addressed was whether the cross-site variations in outcomes could be explained by differences in key program characteristics. In order to assess whether program variations between the intervention and comparison conditions accounted for any of the observed outcome changes, a series of program contrasts were developed and measured. These eight contrasts attempted to capture programmatic differences between the intervention and comparison conditions at each site on a number of dimensions related to the intervention. One program contrast in particular, *Integrated Counseling*, was significantly related to three of the four outcomes measured across the sites. This program-level variable measured how many of the three key treatment foci — mental health, post-traumatic symptoms and substance abuse — women reported receiving. Treatment sites where there were high contrasts between the intervention and comparison conditions showed a larger effect size on four outcome variables. These findings suggest that the effects of the interventions are conditioned on providing integrated counseling to women who have co-occurring disorders. A second program contrast significantly related to improvement in outcomes was the number of core services received in the treatment program. Considering the two significant program contrasts together, sites in which women received more services did not produce better results than their comparison counterparts unless they also received more integrated counseling services. This finding appears to underscore the importance of integrating of mental health, substance abuse and trauma treatment for women with co-occurring disorders.

Cocozza et al. (2005) identified a number of limitations to this study that caution against drawing firm conclusions. First, the study relied on a quasi-experimental, non-random design that occurred within the context of a large, multi-site trial. Second, intervention conditions were consistent in their key program characteristics, but varied greatly in actual programs and services implemented to meet them. Third, comparison conditions were also not uniform and not static. Fourth, tasks in the comparison condition were not provided the federal funds to enhance services based on the intervention model being tested. Anecdotal information suggests that some comparison sites began incorporating elements of trauma-specific interventions over the life of the study. Fifth, the use of a prospective meta-analytic approach and program contrast is well suited to a study involving multiple sites with varied interventions. Yet these methods are relatively new (Banks et al., 2002) and procedures for developing and measuring program contrasts can and should be improved over the strategies employed in the WCDVS. Nonetheless, the results presented here support the usefulness of trauma informed treatment approaches. approach. Sixth, two of the eight program contrasts explained variability in outcomes, increased understanding of the conditions under which the interventions work. These two contrasts were based on client self-reports of services received, whereas the other six contrasts were based on ratings completed by informants from the intervention sites, who were not blinded to study hypotheses or study conditions, thus raising questions regarding the impact of the measurement itself. Finally, the findings reported here are based on 6-month outcome data. Whether these initial findings hold up over the full 12-month follow-up period will be addressed in subsequent papers. Despite these limitations, the findings suggest that outcomes for women with multiple and interrelated needs can be improved by comprehensive, integrated, trauma-informed, and CSR-involved services and that these effects are much more pronounced when services emphasize integrated counseling.

Results from the Morrissey et al. (2005) study, found no effect for substance use outcomes. However, the meta-analysis demonstrated small, but statistically significant overall improvements in trauma and mental health symptomology in the intervention relative to the usual-care comparison condition. Analysis of key program elements demonstrated that integrating substance abuse, mental health, and trauma-related issues into counseling yielded greater improvement, whereas delivery of numerous core services yielded less improvement relative to the comparison group.

Morrissey, et al. (2005) noted the following limitation to their study: Because this was an intent-to-treat analysis, it did not include information about the actual amount of services received by participants in the intervention and comparison groups. Therefore, the writers were unable to compare across sites and conditions the proportion of participants enrolled and retained in-group interventions or the dosage received. It is possible that the reported intervention and program contrast effects may be due in part to differences in enrollment, engagement, retention, or dosage. Second, measures of integrated counseling and core services relied on self-reported data, which were not validated in conjunction with attendance data. Third, participants' ratings of integrated counseling may be related to their level of symptoms. Morrissay et al. suggest that research should focus on the direct measurement of integrated counseling and other program-level factors through logs or other service records. Finally, although the meta-analysis controlled for some baseline differences, this study used a quasi-experimental design. Any of the effects detected may be due in part to baseline differences between participants in different study conditions or program contrast conditions or due to imperfections in the rigorous but admittedly arbitrary methods used to control for measured differences. The use of randomized designs in future research would overcome a number of these constraints.

Despite these limitations, the 12-month outcome data suggests that women with severe symptoms, a history of violence and trauma, and co-occurring disorders may benefit from these integrated trauma-informed and trauma-specific interventions.

Seeking Safety and *Women's Integrated Treatment* (WIT) are examples of trauma-informed and trauma-specific therapy models that have proven effective in treating women who experience complex co-occurring disorders and trauma histories (Hien, Campbett, Ruglass, Miechen, & Killeen, 2010).

Seeking Safety

Seeking Safety is a manual-based training designed to address posttraumatic stress disorder among individuals with substance used disorders (Najavits, 2002). The *Seeking Safety* model is a 25-session cognitive-behavior therapy that is based on five key principles: (a) safety as the priority; (b) integrated treatment of Posttraumatic Stress Disorder (PTSD) and substance abuse conjointly; (c) a focus on ideals; (e) four content areas - - cognitive, behavioral, interpersonal and case management; and (f) attention to the therapist processes. Each session is designed to address a coping skill relevant to PTSD and substance abuse. Sample topics include honesty, asking for help, setting boundaries in relationships, and recovery thinking (Najavits, Weiss & Liese, 1996). Foundational to successful integration of the model is comprehensive staff training that includes didactic education regarding PTSD and substance use disorders and therapeutic intervention skills. Empathetic response (soothing the client through acknowledging and reflecting the client's feelings and emotional pain, initiating connecting responses such as "I see", Oh, that must feel..." and paraphrasing the content of what the client is saying) is considered one of the fundamental counseling skills necessary for administering the model (Najavitis, 2005; McShaw & Glenow, 2000).

Hien et al. (2010) conducted a secondary analysis of a NIDA Clinical Trials Network Study, "Women and Trauma Study", that explored the effectiveness of two interventions for women with co-occurring PTSD and substance use disorders. The original study took place in seven community-based intensive outpatient substance abuse treatment programs located throughout the United States. It studied 353 females, ages 18-65, with at least one lifetime traumatic event and who met DSM-IV criteria for either full or sub-threshold PTSD in the past 30 days. Sub-threshold PTSD differs from full PTSD in that participants could meet either criterion C (avoidance of trauma reminders and emotional numbing) or criterion D (hyper-arousal), but not both as in the full diagnostic requirement. Treatment interventions included *Seeking Safety* (Najavits, 2002) and *Women's Health Education* (Miller, 1998). Hien et al.'s (2010) study explored the validity of the findings in the initial study. The authors felt that the initial study, whose overall findings did not provide support for the superiority of trauma-specific therapy over an active health education curriculum, was influenced by inclusion criteria that only required substance use in the past six months. Thus, all of the participants were abstinent at enrollment. The authors contend that the findings may render a more accurate result if participants were actively using substances at the time of enrollment.

The secondary study consisted of a subset of 274 participants from the original clinical trial who identified active substance use as a baseline. Their analysis captured the prior 30 days of substance use. Treatment changes were modeled to examine posttraumatic stress disorder symptomatology and substance use changes over the six treatment weeks, and secondarily, the impact of treatment response (i.e., clinically significant PTSD or substance use symptom change during the treatment phase) during follow-up. Findings revealed significant benefits on substance use outcomes over the 12-month follow-up for participants in trauma-focused treatment who had more severe substance use at the start of treatment and who experienced reductions in their PTSD symptoms as a result of treatment. This analysis highlights the importance of assessing pre-treatment symptom characteristics and in-treatment symptom change processes, both of which influence treatment outcomes.

Furthermore, for women using alcohol, PTSD symptom scores were significantly lower in the *Seeking Safety* intervention during treatment and follow-up. Baseline alcohol users in the *Seeking Safety* group who had higher baseline hyper-arousal severity improved more quickly than those with lower baseline hyper-arousal severity. Among those with no alcohol misuse at baseline, there were no differences in PTSD outcomes at the end of treatment or during the follow-up period. All participants benefited from the interventions (i.e., a reduction in PTSD symptoms regardless of the intervention (i.e., Seeking Safe or Women's Health Education, Hien, et. al.). These findings suggest that identifying the nature and scope of substance use at treatment entry may be an important factor in determining treatment selection among those with co-occurring PTSD and substance use disorders. Further, the scope and/or frequency of alcohol use prior to or at the time of admission may indicate a more severe clinical presentation for those with co-occurring trauma histories. These findings support prior research, which suggests specific alcohol severity and trauma symptom cluster relationships (Black, Sonne, Kileen, Dansky & Brady., 2003; Taft, Resick, Watkins & Panuzio, 2009). Seeking safety was found to be effective in addressing the severity and these confounding interactions between substance use and trauma symptoms (Taft, et al., 2009).

The International Society for Traumatic Stress Studies Practice Guidelines (2009) identifies *Seeking Safety* as the only effective treatment model for co-occurring PTSD and substance use disorders. However, Hein et. al. (2010) contends that *Seeking Safety* is more an early stage treatment model, which is most appropriate for those who are actively using and have high symptom severity. Later stage trauma therapies such as Cognitive Processing Therapy or Prolonged Exposure Therapy are more appropriate for those whose substance use disorder has stabilized and who are not actively engaging in substance use.

Women's Integrated Treatment Model (WIT)

Addressing the need for integrated trauma services with women, Covington et al. (2008) developed a gender responsive, trauma-specific treatment model called the *Women's Integrated Treatment Model* (WIT). The model contains a manualized curriculum, *Helping Women Recover* and *Beyond Trauma*. The curricula are grounded in theories of addiction, trauma, and women's psychological healthcare.

Helping Women Recover

Helping Women Recover provides an integrated manualized curriculum for treating women with histories of addiction and trauma. It is designed for use in a variety of settings, including outpatient and residential substance abuse treatment programs, domestic violence shelters, mental health clinics, jails, prisons and community corrections facilities. *Helping Women Recover* is founded on research, clinical practice, and is grounded in the theories of addiction, trauma, and women's psychological development. These theories are applied using psycho-educational, cognitive-behavioral, expressive arts, and relational approaches. Addiction and trauma theories create the basis of the seventeen-session program. The sessions are divided into four modules: Self, Relationships, Sexuality, and Spirituality (Covington, et al., 2008) The above modules are common triggers for women in early recovery (Covington, 1994).

Beyond Trauma: A Healing Journey for Women

Beyond Trauma is a manualized curriculum for women's treatment. It is based on theory, research, and clinical practice (Covington, 2003). The materials present in *Beyond Trauma* are trauma-specific. The connection between trauma and substance abuse is recognized and integrated throughout the curriculum. Three modules include eleven sessions focused on violence, abuse and trauma, the impact of trauma, and healing from trauma. Similar to *Helping Women Recover*, *Beyond Trauma* is designed for use in outpatient, residential, and criminal justice settings. It is intended for use alone or in conjunction with *Helping Women Recover*.

The major emphasis is on coping skills and utilizing specific exercises for developing emotional wellness. Additionally, *Beyond Trauma* has a psycho-educational component that teaches women what trauma is, its process, and its impact on the inner-self (thoughts, feelings, beliefs, and values) and the outer self (behavior and relationships, including parenting). Through cognitive-behavioral techniques (CBT), expressive arts, and the principles of relational therapy, *Beyond Trauma* assists women in learning to deal with expression and containment of feelings as they move toward emotional wellness.

While it is recommended that the curriculum be utilized sequentially, it can be implemented independently. Each session includes an overview of the materials to be covered, a group check-in, a teaching component and an interactive component, and a closing that includes questions for the women to think about prior to the next session (Covington, 2003).

Covington et al. (2008) evaluated the effectiveness of *Women's Integrated Treatment* (WIT) in a 12-month Residential treatment facility for adult women (ages 18-54) including those with children. The treatment program was based on a social treatment model; that is, staff model appropriate behavior and rely on peer influence to help participants to achieve sobriety and individual goals. The majority of staff members at the study site were former program participants. Over half of the 157 participants were mandated to treatment, and the population was ethnically diverse (41% Caucasian, 31% Hispanic or Latino, 18% African American, 10% Asian, American). The women possessed limited educational resources (42% had completed high school or GED), and lacked stable housing. In the study, *Helping Women Recover* and *Beyond Trauma* curriculum were presented sequentially.

Women who successfully completed the WIT program were assessed at several stages of treatment (intake, completion of the first 45 days, completion of *How Women Recover* and *Beyond Trauma*, and upon treatment exit). Assessments measured addiction severity, trauma symptomatology and depression. The *Addiction Severity Index for Females* (ASI-F; SAMHSA 1999) was used to assess the criminal and mental health histories of the clients. The ASI-F measures the severity of drug and alcohol use and five related problem areas (family/social, legal, psychological, employment and medical).

Trauma symptomology was evaluated using the *Trauma Symptom Checklist* (TSC-40; Elliott & Briere, 1992). The TSC-40 is a 40-item, self-reporting instrument that assesses symptomology in adults associated with childhood or adult trauma - - in particular, symptoms of posttraumatic stress disorder (PTSD). It consists of six subscales: Anxiety, Dissociation, Depression, Sexual Abuse Trauma Index (SATI), Sleep Disturbance, and Sexual Problems. Each symptom item is rated according to its frequency of occurrence over the prior two months, using a four-point scale ranging from 0 ("never") to 3 ("often"). Studies using the TSC-40 indicate that it is a relatively reliable measure (subscale alphas typically range from .66 to .77, with alphas for the full scale averaging between .89 and .91; Dunn, Ryan & Dunn, 1994).

Characteristics and symptoms of depression were measured by the Beck Depression Inventory (BDI; Beck et al., 1961), a 21-item self-report rating inventory that measures characteristic attitudes and symptoms of depression. Internal consistency for the BDI ranges from .73 to.92, with a mean of .86, and with alpha coefficients of .86 and .81 for psychiatric and non-psychiatric populations, respectively (Beck, Steer & Garbin, 1988).

Covington (2008) noted several limitations of the study. First, the funding emphasis of for this project was focused on service delivery. Therefore research funds were limited. Second, research funding limitations resulted in a reliance on program staff members (who lacked research experience and who had other program responsibilities) to collect the data and to locate clients and conduct follow-up assessments. Third, there was no comparison group as the study contained a sample of convenience. Fourth, the studies small sample size limits the generalizability of the findings. Efforts were made by the research staff to mitigate the impact of these limitations. To increase the integrity of the data set, the research staff reviewed case files and forms, created data-entry forms on Survey Monkey (an online data-entry service), created systems to assist the staff in keeping track of data time points, attended monthly meetings with the program staff to discuss issues, and provided written feedback to the staff about their forms. However, there was not the level of standardization that would have occurred if the data had been collected by the research staff. As a result, there were issues with the standardization of data collected, amount of data collected, and qualitative data interpretation. In addition, because the attrition rate from intake to exit provided a small sample of convenience, comprised of those clients who were available and agreed to participate, the data that were received should be viewed with caution.

Despite these limitations, the findings indicated that women who completed the *Women's Integrated Treatment* curriculum components evidenced significant decrease in depression ($p < .05$) and fewer trauma symptoms, ($p < .05$) including anxiety, sleep disturbances and dissociation after completion.

Seeking Safety and *Women's Integrated Treatment* (WIT) approaches encourage integration of positive coping strategies as a goal in recovery. Identified interventions employ cognitive behavior and relational interventions that are not by intent religiously or spiritually based. However, the inclusion of positive relational aspects in these two approaches supports the relational components of Fowler's Faith Development theory.

Chapter Summary

The preceding chapter provides a comprehensive review of the theoretical and empirical literature associated with spiritual development theory, and trauma theory. The inclusive review of the literature reinforced the multifarious challenges that accompany the co-occurrence of mental health disorders and trauma among women with substance use disorders (Kauffman, Silver, & Poulin, 1997; Najavitis, 2005;Tuchman, 2010) Further, comprehensive trauma-specific and trauma-informed treatment approaches for addressing co-occurring trauma and substance use disorders in women were examined (*Seeking Safety* and *Women's Integrated Treatment;* Covington et al., 2008; Najavitis, 2005).

Additionally, the mitigating components of integrated spiritual constructs and individualized spiritual practices in posttraumatic growth and recovery from co-occurring disorders were established. (Tuchman, 2010; Smith et al., 2003; Vis & Boynton, 2008). Due to the lack of research concerning the impact of trauma on the spiritual development of women with substance use disorders, this study explored the nature of the relationship between trauma and the spiritual development of women with substance use disorders.

Chapter Three describes the design and methodology of the study including: the population and sample, data collection procedures, instrumentation, research design and data analysis. Ethical considerations of the study are also examined.

CHAPTER 3

METHODOLOGY

Introduction

This chapter details the methodological approach used in this study. Included in this chapter is the description of the research question/sub-questions; the data source; rationale for the research designs, including population, sample and sampling procedures; study procedures; and instrumentation. A description of the statistical analysis used to examine the research question and sub-questions as well as ethical considerations, concludes this chapter.

Research Questions

The purpose of this exploratory study was to examine the relationship between trauma and the spiritual well-being in women with substance use disorders. Specifically, this study explored the following research question and sub-questions:

What is the relationship between type of trauma and spiritual well-being, in women with substance abuse disorders when comparing different types of trauma?

Sub-question A: What is the relationship between age of first traumatic occurrence and spiritual well-being in women with substance use disorders as measured by the Spiritual Well-Being Scale and the Trauma Assessment?

Sub-question B: What is the relationship between the number of traumatic occurrences and the spiritual well-being in women with substance use disorders as measured by the *Spiritual Well-Being Scale* and the *Trauma Assessment*?

Archival Data and Definition of Variables

This study utilizes archival data collected from a comprehensive gender inclusive study examining the *Impact of Trauma on the Spiritual Development of Individuals with Substance*

Use Disorders. The initial study contained males and females enrolled in a comprehensive, multi-year, modified therapeutic community who met DSM IV-R diagnostic criteria for a substance use disorder. The present study reflects gender specific data obtained from female residents with more than thirty consecutive days enrolled in the modified therapeutic community. The primary advantage for using archival data is the ability to examine information collected over a 24-month period that included individuals at various stages of program involvement. The primary disadvantage of using archival data is the inability to gather missing data from study participants. Data was collected from April 2010 to August 2012. Demographic information included: age, legal history, drug of preference, employment status prior to admission, housing prior to admission, and program admission date. Data were obtained from the agency database, Demographic Information Sheet, the *Adapted Trauma Assessment*, and the *Spiritual Well-Being* (SWB) *Scale*.

For statistical analysis, demographic information as well as data obtained from the research instruments was entered into (SPSS) release version 18.0.0 program (SPSS: An IBM Company, 2009). Participants who did not complete all items on the study instruments were not included in the statistical analysis. There was no specific subset of women identified who failed to complete all of the questions. Therefore, missing data was assumed to be random in occurrence rather than the result of deliberate omission. Of the 115 participants eligible for the study, missing and/or omitted data on one or more of the assessment instruments was present for seven of the consenting participants. There were 108 participants with no missing data. Therefore, they constituted the sample.

Definition of Variables

For the purpose of this study, the variables were defined as follows:

Demographic variables: Refers to participants' stated gender, age, ethnicity, and highest level of education completed, legal history, military history, and program entry date/length of time in the program, age of first alcohol use, length of time the individual has used alcohol, age at first drug use, length of time the individual has used drugs (other than alcohol), primary drug of use, previous diagnosis, treatment interventions received prior to entering the modified therapeutic community, and current treatment interventions they are receiving as part of their current care.

Substance Use Disorder: Refers to the DSM IV-R diagnostic criteria for substance abuse and dependence. For the purposes of this study, individuals meeting a substance dependence diagnosis were included.

Therapeutic Community: Refers to a treatment approach for substance use disorders that incorporates a highly structured daily regimen; fosters personal responsibility and self-help in managing life difficulties; utilizes peers as role models with the peer community acting as the healing agent within a strategy of community-as-method (the community provides both the context for and mechanism of change); regards change as a gradual, developmental process and directs clients through progressive treatment stages; stresses work and self-reliance through the development of vocational and independent living skills; and promotes pro-social values within healthy social networks to sustain recovery (Sacks, Banks, McKendrick & Sacks, 2008).

Modified Therapeutic Community: Refers to a treatment approach that maintains the key elements, structure, and processes of the standard Therapeutic Community model, but is designed to accommodate individual needs, impairments, and deficits of clients with co-occurring disorders (Sacks, Banks, McKendrick & Sacks, 2008).

Research Design

This exploratory study examined the relationship between trauma and the spiritual well-being of women with substance use disorders. The exploratory nature of this study: (a) provided descriptive data regarding the sample of interest; (b) provided the flexibility to employ archival data; (c) broadened existing, yet limited, research on the topic of trauma on the spiritual well-being of substance abusing women. Specifically, the impact of age of first occurrence and the impact of single verses multiple traumatic occurrences on spiritual well-being; (d) allowed simultaneous investigation of multiple research questions; (e) permitted the examination of number of variables; (f) directed and refined future research inquiries; and (g) assisted in determining the best approach in reaching research (Cresswell, 2009; Grove & Anderson, 1982).

Population

Participants for this study were adult female residents of a two-year modified therapeutic community in Durham, North Carolina, who had at least thirty consecutive days enrolled in the program. Participants included in the study met admission criteria for this modified therapeutic community (individuals 18 years or older, possess a history of a substance use disorder, medically and psychiatrically stable, and meet the American Society of Addiction Medicine (ASAM) criteria for inpatient treatment). English was the primary language for all participants.

As previously noted, the treatment approach in a modified therapeutic community upholds the key elements, structure, and processes of the standard Therapeutic Community (TC) model, but is designed to accommodate the complex needs of residents with co-occurring disorders (Sacks, et al., 2008). In contrast to 12-step or other spiritually based programs, the Therapeutic Community or Modified Therapeutic Community model endorses a social learning, community-as-method philosophy. Community accountability, rather than spiritual understanding, is the primary agent of change. Employment, work ethic, and self-empowerment, within the context of healthy social networks and pro-social values are the foundational elements for sustained recovery (Sacks, et al., 2008). Spiritual and/or religious considerations are not direct components of the therapeutic milieu.

Sample and Sampling

Participant selection was achieved via selective sampling method. Selective sampling contains individuals who are deliberately chosen using a sampling plan that selects only those with relevant characteristics (Heppner, et al., 2008). In the case of this study, eligible participants were female residents with a diagnosed substance use disorder admitted to the two-year modified therapeutic community. The use of selective sampling allows the inclusion of members of the population that were willing to participate in the study. Support for this sampling method is noted by Serlin (1987).

From the data set 115 participants consented for participation in the study and matched eligibility requirements. Only 108 participants were included in the study as there was missing and/or omitted data on one or more of the assessment instruments for three of the residents who consented to participation in the study.

Procedures

Each participant completed three self-report questionnaires (*Supplemental Demographic Information, Adapted Trauma Assessment*, and *Spiritual Well-Being Scale)* as part of their study participation. The questionnaires were completed in a single session, lasting up to 90 minutes. There was no planned follow up. Consideration was given to the language and sequencing of study instrumentation in order to provide clear directions in soliciting the most accurate information from participants. Questions on the *Adapted Trauma Assessment* were written at a reading level consistent with recommendations for patient materials (6th grade, McHugh, Rasmussen, & Otto, 2011). Items related to physical and sexual abuse included behavioral explanations in order to provide definitional clarity and item standardization. Assessment Packets were ordered with the *Supplemental Demographic Information* followed by *Trauma Assessment* and then the *Spiritual Well-Being Scale*.

Data Collection

Eligibility for initial study involvement was established based on information provided in the participants' initial screening as well as the intake assessment completed at the time of admission to the therapeutic community. Eligible participants met with the study investigator to review the purpose and parameters of the study as well to verify the East Carolina University (ECU) Institutional Review Board (IRB) approved informed consent for research, and HIPAA notification documentation (Appendix E). Individuals that provided consent completed a *Supplemental Demographic Information* (Appendix A), *Adapted Trauma Assessment* (Appendix B), and *Spiritual Well-Being Scale* (Appendix C). Individual instruments are discussed in more detail in the instrumentation section. To address any unexpected emotional concerns or reactions that might arise in response to answering trauma related questions, staff counselors were available to participants for debriefing and follow up.

Instrumentation

A series of self-report reporting measures were selected to examine the impact of trauma on the spiritual development of women with substance use disorders. As previously noted, study measures were completed in one administration, lasting up to 90 minutes.

Demographic Information

Demographic information was obtained from the agency database and a *Supplemental Demographic Information* form. The *Supplemental Demographic Information* form is a two-page researcher-developed demographic survey (Appendix A). Demographic information provided from the agency data base reflected responses provided in the participant's intake screening and in their completed psychosocial assessment. Information collected from the database included: (a) age, (b) race, (c) program entry date, (d) length of stay in treatment, (e) highest grade completed, (f) number of incarcerations, (g) number of felony arrests, (h) number of misdemeanor arrests, (i) homelessness, and (j) military history. Information gained from the *Supplemental Demographic Information* form included: (a) gender, (b) age (c) race, (d) treatment entry date/length of time in treatment (e) age of first alcohol use, (f) length of alcohol use, (g) age of first drug use, (h) length of drug use, (i) drug of preference, (j) veteran status, (k) legal history, (l) types of treatment/counseling received had in the past, (m) services received since entering the current program, and (n) previous/current diagnosis.

Spiritual Well-Being Scale

Ellison's (1983) *Spiritual Well-Being* scale (SWBS) is a self-report questionnaire with 20 items assessing spirituality, which are rated on a 6-point Likert scale ranging from 1 (strongly agree) to 6 (strongly disagree). This measure is nonsectarian; therefore, it can be used with people from a wide range of beliefs and backgrounds. The SWBS has been used in studies of male–female differences, senior citizens, religious and nonreligious individuals, respondents from rural and city areas, and the chronically ill (Ellison, 1983; Miller, 2003)

The SWBS generates an overall Spiritual Well-Being score (SWB), an Existential Well-Being score (EWB) and a Religious Well-Being score (RWB). Existential Well-Being scores range from 20 to 60. The EWB score reflects a participant's level of life perspective and purpose. Individuals with high EWB scores have a sense of their connection to others and a sense of shared meaning. Religious Well-Being scores range from 10 to 60, with higher scores suggesting a greater level of religious well-being. Individuals with high RWB scores have a sense of their connection to the divine. The overall or total score (SWB) is a composite of the RWB and EWB, ranging from 40 to 120, which provides a measure of overall level of spirituality. Higher scores within each of the spirituality domains (i.e., SWB, EWB, RWB) indicate greater overall spiritual well-being.

The utility of the Spiritual Well-Being Scale as a psychometrically sound predictor of spiritual well-being among diverse demographic groups and in a variety of healthcare settings has been established (Ellison and Smith, 1991). The test- retest reliability for the SWBS is 0.93. The reliabilities for the RWB and EWB subscales are 0.96 and 0.86 respectively. Correlations for the subscales of the SWBS are $r = 0.32$. This confirms that the sub scales are testing separate aspects of spiritual well-being (Ellison and Smith 1991). Ellison (1982) reported that the correlation between the subscales for the 20-item version of the scale was .32 ($p < .001$), the correlation between SWB and RWB was ($r = 90$). The correlation between SWB and EWB was ($r = .59$). Concurrent validity is difficult to determine due to the limited number of measures of spiritual well-being (D'Costa, 1995).

For this study Cronbach's alpha reliability of the 20-item Spiritual Well-Being Scale revealed overall or total spiritual well-being (after reverse scoring for the appropriate items) was .94 indicating high internal reliability. Sub-groups of existential well-being and religious well-being were .88 and .94 respectively.

Trauma Assessment

Trauma history was measured by a researcher *Adapted Traumatic Life Events Questionnaire (A-TLEQ)* The TLEQ is one of the most recognized and respected trauma assessment instruments (Elhai, Gray, Kashdan, & Franklin, 2005). A self-report scale, the TLEQ assesses exposure to 21 types of potentially traumatic events. An open-ended category addresses exposure to "other events". Examples consistent with *Diagnostic and Statistical Manual IV* posttraumatic stress disorder criterion A-1 are included. Traumatic and/or disturbing events are described in behaviorally descriptive terms. Emotionally charged terms such as *rape* or *abuse* are avoided. For acknowledged events, respondents are asked to indicate the number of times the event occurred on a seven-point scale ranging from never to five times or more. Participants are asked whether each event evoked fear, helplessness, or horror. Additional questions ask about physical injury and immediate emotional response to the event. Finally, in the case of exposure to multiple events, respondents are asked to indicate which event they perceive as the worst. The TLEQ can be administered in 10 to 15 minutes. Although brief, the inclusiveness of the TLEQ is effective in identifying forms of traumatic experiences not assessed in structured trauma assessment interview. One study found that 93% of participants completing the TLEQ reported exposure to at least one traumatic event; while 69% of participants being assessed by a structured interview trauma history assessment reported exposure to at least one traumatic event, indicating strong content validity (Kubany et al., 2000).

Psychometric properties were evaluated in a multi-sample, multi-study report (Kubany et al., 2000). Sample scores and norms related to the occurrence of traumatic events across five samples are presented. The temporal stability of the TLEQ was evaluated in a sample of 42 battered women. Kappa coefficients assessing agreement over 2 weeks were above .40 for 20 of the 21 items and .60 or above for 12 items. The overall mean percentage of test-retest agreement was 86%. Correlations of frequency of occurrence reports for each event (with the exception of combat) averaged .77 and ranged from .50 to .93. The test-retest reliability of the occurrence or nonoccurrence of criterion A-2 (intense fear, helplessness, and horror) yielded kappa coefficients of .40 or higher for 19 of the 21 items and .60 or higher for 16 items. The overall percentage of agreement for criteria A-2 was 89%.

Seven experts in the area of PTSD rated relevance and representativeness of several aspects of the TLEQ (e.g., response format, individual items) for measuring PTSD as defined in DSMIV-R. Overall, item wording was rated very positively, as was adequacy of coverage for traumatic events.

Convergent validity was assessed in a sample of 62 undergraduate students. Agreement was evaluated between a self-report and interview version of a slightly modified version of the TLEQ. Kappa coefficients were .40 for 15 of the 16 items and above .60 for 13 items. This would suggest that there was greater agreement for thirteen of the sixteen items surveyed. The overall mean percentage of agreement was 92%. Convergent validity was also assessed for the two formats administered one week apart with similar, but slightly lower, agreement. All but one Vietnam veteran with documented service records endorsed exposure to combat. Among women reporting a history of battery, 98% of those who met cut off criteria for a PTSD diagnosis indicated that they had experienced partner abuse with fear, helplessness, and horror at the time of the event. Discriminative validity was assessed in a sample of women who met parameters for *PTSD* on a self-report measure and who reported significantly more categories of traumatic events, more total events, and more events that evoked intense fear, helplessness, and horror on the TLEQ than women who did not meet the PTSD cutoff.

Trauma related variables for this study were measured by a researcher adapted version of the *Traumatic Life Events Questionnaire* (Elhai, Gray, Kashdan, & Franklin, 2005). The *Adapted Trauma Assessment* (Appendix C), in keeping with the TLEQ, is a self-report measure that assesses exposure to multiple forms of potentially traumatic events consistent with *Diagnostic and Statistical Manual IV* posttraumatic stress disorder criterion A-1. Traumatic and/or disturbing events are described in behavioral terms. Endorsed events address frequency of occurrence. The modified *Trauma Assessment* identifies ten forms of potentially traumatic events. Additionally, the frequency of specified trauma occurrences is reduced from six occurrences on the TLEQ to three on the adapted version. Individuals who identify more than three occurrences are coded as "four or more traumas". The *Adapted Trauma Assessment* expands data collected in the TLEQ through the inclusion of the age of occurrence/s and classification of the offender (stranger, friend/acquaintance, family member, partner/spouse, self or other). Additionally, the modified assessment includes differentiation and definitional descriptions for three separate forms of sexual trauma (i.e. attempted rape, completed rape, molestation). Adaptation of the TLEQ supports delineation among the nature/type of traumatic events to which respondents have been exposed, while expanding the data in a manner that permits comparison of the types of trauma occurrence, frequency of trauma occurrence and age of occurrence consistent with the stated research questions. Although brief, the inclusiveness of the *Adapted Trauma Assessment,* is effective in identifying forms of traumatic experiences not assessed in structured trauma assessment interview.

This study utilized an *Adapted Trauma Assessment* (A-TLEQ, Appendix C). In keeping with the TLEQ, the adapted assessment is a self-report measure that assesses exposure to multiple forms of potentially traumatic events consistent with *Diagnostic and Statistical Manual*

IV posttraumatic stress disorder criterion A-1. Traumatic and/or disturbing events are described in behaviorally descriptive terms. Endorsed events address frequency of occurrence. The modified *Trauma Assessment* combines forms of trauma resulting from natural disaster, accidents, combat, and physical illness into one-item. Additionally, the frequency of specified trauma occurrences is reduced from six on the TLEQ to three on the modified version. The modified *Trauma Assessment* expands data collected in the TLEQ through the inclusion of the age of occurrence/s and classification of the offender (stranger, friend/acquaintance, family member, partner/spouse, self or other). Additionally, the modified assessment includes differentiation and definitional descriptions for three separate forms of sexual trauma (i.e. attempted rape, completed rape, molestation). Adaptation of the TLEQ supports the delineation of the nature of traumatic events to which respondents have been exposed, while expanding the data in a manner that permits comparison of varieties of trauma and age of occurrence consistent with the stated research question.

Statistical Analyses

Research Question and Sub-questions: What is the relationship between type of trauma and spiritual well-being, in women with substance abuse disorders when comparing different types of trauma?

Sub-question A: What is the relationship between age of first traumatic occurrence and spiritual well-being in women with substance use disorders as measured by the *Spiritual Well-Being Scale* and the *Trauma Assessment*?

Sub-question B: What is the relationship between the number of traumatic occurrences and the spiritual well-being in women with substance use disorders as measured by the *Spiritual Well-Being Scale* and the *Trauma Assessment*?

For this study, the dependent variable was the spiritual well-being score. Independent variables were the type of trauma occurrence, age of first traumatic occurrence, and the number of traumatic occurrences. To determine the nature of the relationships between the variables, a descriptive, correlational research design was chosen (Cresswell, 2013; Issac & Michael, 1995). To address the research question Independent *t*-tests were used to compare mean differences of Spiritual Well-Being scores for the various types of trauma. To further examine the impact of type of trauma on the Spiritual Well-Being score (SWB), a simultaneous (all ten predictor variables grouped together) multiple linear regression analysis was conducted to determine if spiritual well-being scores could be predicted based on the nature of the trauma experienced by the participants. Correlational analysis and a simultaneous (all ten predictor variables grouped together) multiple linear regression analysis were used to address research sub-questions A and B. Further, correlational analysis and a simultaneous multiple linear regression analysis supported exploration of the relationship between the number of trauma occurrences on the "intrinsic" and "extrinsic", spiritual well-being scores as measured by the *Trauma Assessment* and the *Spiritual Well-Being Scale*.

All tests were two-tailed, given that there was no definitive direction indicated in literature. Significance level was set at 0.05, which has been reported as a customary alpha level for social science research (Witte & Witte, 1997).

Ethical Considerations

East Carolina University IRB approval to conduct research was obtained. In terms of participant privacy, ethical considerations were ensured through the analysis and reporting of data in the proposed study. Coded identifiers were used in the study, linking personal information of each participant to his or her specific identifier; however, information such as name, address, and phone number are not required for the purposes of this study. Therefore, coded identifier were linked to demographic and evaluation data only, minimizing the risk of privacy infringement.

Chapter Summary

The research design and methodology support the purpose of this study, which examined the relationship between trauma and the spiritual well-being in women with substance use disorders. Specifically, this study explored whether the level of trauma is associated with the level of spiritual well-being of women with substance use disorders. Limitations of the research design deal with issues around interpretation. The exploratory nature of this study inhibits the inclusion causal inferences. Additionally, sample size in single-site social science research for women with substance use disorders tends to be limited (Weinberger, McKee & Mazure, 2010). Smaller single-site sample sizes may be reflective of barriers that limit women's access to safe, appropriate clinical treatment as well as gender-specific gaps in clinical research studies in the area of substance abuse and trauma (Weinberger, et al., 2011).

Sample Demographics, Descriptive Statistics, Data Analysis, Exploration of the Relationships found among Variables, and Summary of the Results.

CHAPTER 4

RESULTS

Introduction to the Chapter

The purpose of this study was to explore the relationship between trauma and spiritual well-being of women with substance use disorders. Specifically, this study explored the relationship between the types of trauma; the age of first traumatic occurrence; the number of traumatic occurrences; and total spiritual well-being score as measured by the *Spiritual Well-Being Scale*. This chapter is organized into six sections: Sampling Procedures, Data Preparation, Sample Demographics, Descriptive Statistics, Data Analysis, Exploration of the Relationships found among Variables, and Summary of the Results.

Sampling Procedures

All the participants in this study were women who reported co-occurring trauma and a diagnosed substance use disorder. The women were residents of a two-year modified therapeutic community. Between April 2010 and August 2012, each participant completed the following self-report questionnaires: *Supplemental Demographic Information* form (Appendix A), *Adapted Trauma Assessment* (Appendix B), and *Spiritual Well-Being Scale* (Appendix C). The questionnaires were completed in a single session lasting up to 90 minutes. During this time, 115 participants completed the questionnaires. Additional demographic information was obtained from the agency database.

Data Preparation

Several steps were taken in data preparation, including deletion of participant identifiers (participant name, treatment identification number, and social security number) from the dataset, removal of participants with no identified trauma history, and exclusion of assessment instruments that contained missing or incomplete items.

For each question on the *Adapted Trauma Assessment* (Appendix B), participants were asked how many times they experienced each type of trauma. Answers were coded according to the number of reported occurrences (0 to 4 and above). All participant answers were recorded and entered into SPSS. The "Total Number of Traumatic Experiences by Each Participant" score was obtained by adding together the number of times each participant reported experiencing each type of trauma

For each spiritual well-being questions on the Spiritual Well-Being Form (Appendix C) the participants were asked to circle the choice that best indicated their agreement or disagreement. The items were rated on a 6-point Likert scale ranging from 1 (strongly agree) to 6 (strongly disagree). The responses generated an Existential Well-Being score (EWB), a Religious Well-Being score (RWB) and a Total Spiritual Well-Being score (SWB). Each participant's answer to questions on the *Spiritual Well-Being Scale* was recorded and entered into SPSS. After the data was cleaned, there were 108 participants with no missing data. Therefore they constituted the study sample.

Descriptive Statistics

Descriptive statistics for the 108 participants are noted in this section.

Gender and Age

The sample consisted of 108 adult females. Participant age ranged from 20 to 61 years, with a mean age of 37, median of 38, and a standard deviation of 10.7.

Race and Ethnicity

Participants were asked to identify which one of the National Institutes of Health endorsed racial/ethnic groups they identified with the most. The results were Caucasian (n = 54; 50%), Black or African American (n = 52; 48%), American Indian or Alaska Native (n = 2, 1.9%), Asian (n = 0), Hispanic or Latino (n = 0), and Native Hawaiian or Other Pacific Islander (n = 0). Of the participants in the study, all but two were either Caucasian or Black/African American.

Education

Participants were asked to identify the number of years of education they had completed. Participant education ranged from 8 to 16 years, with a mean of 11 years, a median of 12 years, and a standard deviation of 1.2 years. Thus, the typical participant for this study had a high school education or equivalent.

Substance Use

Participants were asked to identify the age of their first alcohol use, age of first drug (other than alcohol) use, and primary drug of use. One hundred seven (n = 107) of the 108 participants identified a history of alcohol use. Age of first alcohol use ranged from 4 to 24 years, with a mean of 13.1 years, a median of 14.0 years, and a standard deviation of 4.6 years. Thus, the typical participant in this study began using alcohol between the age of 13 and 14. This suggests that the onset of alcohol use occurred in the 7th or 8th grade assuming normal educational progression.

One hundred six (n = 106) of the 108 participants identified a history of drug (other than alcohol) use. Age of first drug use ranged from 9 to 24 years, with a mean of 16 years, median of 15.0 years, and a standard deviation of 3.5 years. Thus, the typical participant commenced drug (other than alcohol) use during the high school years.

Participants were asked to identify their primary drug of use. Primary substance of use from most to least represented was: Cocaine (n = 44; 41%), Alcohol (n = 27; 25%), Opiates (n = 26; 24%), Marijuana (n = 6; 6%), and Methamphetamines (n = 4; 4%). Thus the most frequently identified drug of use was cocaine.

Trauma Exposure

Data from the *Adapted Trauma Assessment* examines participant exposure to ten potentially traumatic events. For each event, the frequency of occurrence, age of occurrence/s, and classification of the offender (friend/acquaintance, family member [other than partner or spouse], partner/spouse, self, stranger or other) was gathered.

Type of Trauma

Participants utilized the *Adapted Trauma Asse*ssment to identify types of trauma/s experienced. Of the 108 participants, the types of trauma reported from most to least represented were: Completed Rapes (n = 74; 69%), Physical Assault (n = 73; 68%) Being Tormented, Stalked or Repeatedly Humiliated (n = 66; 61%), Causing harm to another person (n = 63; 58%), Witnessing a Traumatic Event (n = 61; 56%), Sexual Molestation (n = 55; 51%), Attempted Rapes (n = 44; 41%) Accidents (n = 40; 37%), Natural Disaster (n = 22; 20%), Illness (n = 18; 17%) and Combat (n = 0). Thus, traumas resulting from accidents and natural disasters were reported less frequently than traumas perpetrated by another person.

Number of Trauma Occurrences

The number of trauma occurrences ranged from 1 to 26 occurrences, with a mean of 11.2 occurrences per participant, a median of 11.5 occurrences, and a standard deviation of 6 occurrences (Table 3).

Table 2

Age of First Traumatic Occurrence and Frequency of Traumatic Occurrences

	Range	Mean	Median	SD
Age of First Traumatic Occurrence (In Years)	2 - 34	*9.9*	*9.5*	*6.7*
Number of Traumatic Occurrence	1 - 26	*11.2*	*11.5*	*6.1*

Classification of Offender

Participants were asked to classify the offender for each type and incidence of trauma they experienced. Categories of offenders included: family member [other than partner or spouse], friend/acquaintance, partner/spouse, stranger, and other. The category of the offender for the participant's first traumatic occurrence (for each type of trauma) is shown in Table 3. "Partner/Spouse" was the most frequently reported offender for the "First Traumatic Occurrences of Witnessed Trauma"; "Physical Assault"; Trauma from Being Tormented, Stalked, or Repeatedly Humiliated": and "Cause of Harm to Another Person". "Family Member" was the most frequently reported offender for the first traumatic occurrence of sexual molestation. "Friend/Acquaintance" was the most frequently reported offender for the first traumatic occurrence of "Attempted Rape" and "Completed Rape"

Table: 3

Classification of Offender (First Occurrence)

Type of Trauma	Family Member	Friend/ Acquaintance	Partner/ Spouse	Stranger	No Trauma
Witnessing Trauma	12%	12%	*31%	7%	38%
Physical Assault	28%	13%	*35%	9%	15%
Attempted Rape	6%	*16%	5%	14%	59%
Completed Rape	18%	*29%	9%	13%	31%
Sexual Molestation	*27%	19%	1%	4%	49%
Being Tormented	12%	12%	*31%	4%	41%
Causing Harm	1%	8%	*9%	1%	81%

(*Note:* *Most frequently identified offender for each type of trauma).

Spiritual Well-Being Scores

Ellison's (1983) 20 question, self–report *Spiritual Well-Being Scale* (Appendix C) was used to generate an Existential Well-Being score (EWB), a Religious Well-Being Score (RWB), and an overall or Total Spiritual Well-being score (SWB). Participants were asked to rate each question on a 6-point Likert scale ranging from 1 (strongly agree) to 6 (strongly disagree), with higher scores representing more spiritual well-being. Reverse scoring is used for negatively worded items (questions 1, 2, 5, 6, 9, 12, 13, 16, and 18).

Existential Well-Being (EWB) scores range from 20 to 60, with a mean of 46.7, a median of 47.0, and a standard deviation of 9.4. Religious well-being (RWB) scores range from 10 to 60, with a mean of 47.4, a median of 50.5, and a standard deviation of 12.5. Total Spiritual Well-Being scores (SWB) range from 40 to 120, with a mean of 94, a median of 98.5, and a standard deviation of 19.9 (Table 4). The histogram (Figure 2) reveals outliers that may have influenced the distribution of the spiritual well-being scores and subscores.

Table 4

Descriptive Statistics for EWB, RWB and Total SWB

Type of Spiritual Well-Being	Range	Mean	Median	SD
Existential Well-Being (EWB)	20 – 60	46.7	47.0	9.4
Religious Well-Being (RWB)	10 – 60	47.4	50.5	12.5
Spiritual Well-Being (TOTAL)	40 – 120	94.1	98.5	19.8

For each type of trauma, an independent samples t-test was calculated to compare the mean Spiritual Well-Being Score (SWB) of those women who had experienced that type of trauma versus the mean Spiritual Well-Being Score (SWB) of those women who had not experienced that type of trauma. As shown in Table 8, the only type of trauma for which there was a significant difference ($p = .047$) between the mean Spiritual Well-Being score was for women who reported that they had experienced the trauma of sexual molestation (mean Spiritual Well-Being Score = 90.4) versus the mean Spiritual Well-Being score for those women who reported that they had not experienced the trauma of sexual molestation (mean Spiritual Well-Being Score = 97.96). Women who reported experiencing the trauma of sexual molestation had a significantly lower mean Spiritual Well-Being score than those who had not experienced the trauma of sexual molestation.

Table 8

t-Test Results Comparing Mean Spiritual Well-Being Scores With Types of Trauma

Type of Trauma	Mean	SD	*t*	Df	Sig. (2-tailed)
Witnessed Trauma			- .140	105	.889
Not Experienced (n = 32)	93.6	18.73			
Experienced (n = 75)	94.2	20.54			
Trauma from Accident			- .626	106	.533
Not Experienced (n =68)	93.19	19.83			
Experienced (n = 40)	95.68	20.08			
Trauma from Natural Disaster			- 1.04	106	.300
Not Experienced (n = 86)	93.10	19.93			
Experienced (n =22)	98.05	19.57			
Trauma from Illness					
Not Experienced (n =90)	93.12		- 1.16	106	.249
Experienced (n = 40)	99.06	19.95			
		19.19			
Trauma from Physical Assault			- .358	106	.721
Not Experienced (n =15)	92.40	16.08			
Experienced (n = 93)	94.39	20.47			
Trauma from Attempted Rape			.067	106	.947
Not Experienced (n = 65)	94.22	20.65			
Experienced (n = 43)	93.95	19.19			

Trauma from Completed Rape			1.88	106	.063
Not Experienced (n = 34)	99.35	16.83			
Experienced (n = 74)	91.70	20.77			
Trauma from Sexual Molestation			2.01	106	.047*
Not Experienced (n = 53)	97.96	16.81			
Experienced (n = 55)	90.4	21.93			
Trauma from Being Tormented			.298	106	.766
Not Experienced (n = 43)	94.81	18.01			
Experienced (n = 65)	93.65	21.13			
Trauma from Causing Harm to Another			- .055	106	.957
Not Experienced (n = 86)	94.06	20.57			
Experienced (n = 22)	94.32	17.28			

(Note: * Indicates significant results with p-value less than .05)

To examine further the impact of type of trauma on the Spiritual Well-Being score (SWB), a simultaneous (all ten predictor variables grouped together) multiple linear regression analysis was conducted to determine if spiritual well-being scores could be predicted based on the nature of the trauma experienced by the participants (Table 8). The results of the simultaneous multiple linear regression with all ten predictor variables (type of trauma) included revealed no significant linear relationship between any type of trauma and Spiritual Well-Being scores: $R^2 = .109$, $F(11, 95) = 1.06$, $p = .403$.

Table 9

Summary of Multiple Regression Analysis for Type of Trauma and Spiritual Well-Being Scores

	B	SE(B)	*β*	*T*	Sig. (2-tailed) (N=*108*)
Witnessed Trauma	-2.25	4.64	- .052	-.486	.628
Trauma from Accident	2.84	4.60	.069	.671	.538
Trauma from Natural Disaster	5.56	5.13	.113	1.09	.281
Trauma from Illness	7.23	5.96	.136	1.21	.228
Trauma from Physical Assault	5.68	6.07	.099	.935	.352
Trauma from Attempted Rape	-1.15	1.34	-.111	-.856	.394
Trauma from Completed Rape	-10.2	5.35	-.237	-1.91	.060
Trauma from Sexual Molest.	-.675	4.43	-.143	-1.28	.203
Trauma from Being Torment.	-.263	4.40	-.006	-.060	.952
Trauma Causing Harm	4.27	6.67	.087	.641	.523

(Note: $R^2 = .109$)

Research Sub-question:

(a) What is the relationship between the age of first traumatic occurrence and the spiritual well-being score as measured by the *Spiritual Well-Being Scale* and the *Trauma Assessment*?

Bivariate Correlational Analyses were used to examine the relationship between the age of first traumatic experience and Spiritual Well-Being scores (Table 10). For each type of trauma, participants were asked at what age they first experienced that type of trauma.

A significant positive correlation ($r = .215$, $p = .039$) was indicated between the "Age of First Trauma of Physical Assault" and Spiritual Well-Being scores. More specifically, as the participant's age at the time of the first trauma from physical assault increased so did scores on the *Spiritual Well-Being Scale*. Thus, the younger the participant was at the time of their first physical assault, the lower their spiritual well-being score.

A significant positive correlation (r =. 244, p = .048) was indicated between "Age of First Trauma from Being Tormented/Stalked/Repeatedly Humiliated" and Spiritual Well-Being scores. That is, as the participant's age at the time of first trauma of being "Tormented/Stalked/Repeatedly Humiliated" increased, scores on the *Spiritual Well-Being Scale increased*. Thus, the younger the participant was at the time the trauma of being Tormented/Stalked/Repeatedly Humiliated the lower her spiritual well-being score.

Additionally, a significant positive correlation (r = .519, p = .016) was found between "Age of first Causing Harm to Another Person" and Spiritual Well-Being scores. This suggests that the younger the age at the time of causing harm to another person the lower the Spiritual Well-Being score as measured by the *Spiritual Well-Being Scale*. The data yielded no other significant relationships between the participant's age at the time of the remaining types of traumatic occurrences and Spiritual Well-Being scores.

Table 10

Relationship between Age of First Traumatic Occurrence and Total Spiritual Well-Being

Type of Trauma	(*N* =)	Pearson Correlation	Sig (2-tailed)
Age of First Witnessed Trauma	77	-.09	.452
Age of First Trauma from Accident	40	.09	.584
Age of First Trauma from Natural Disaster	22	-.14	.540
Age of First Trauma from Illness	18	.46	.053
Age of First Trauma from Physical Assault	92	.22*	.039
Age of First Trauma from Attempted Rape	44	.18	.248
Age of First Trauma from Completed Rape	74	.08	.502
Age of First Trauma from Sexual Molestat.	55	-.15	.280
Age of First Trauma from Being Tormented	66	.24*	.048*
Age of First Causing Harm to Another	21	.52*	.016*

(Note: * Indicates significant results with p-value less than .05)

Supplementary Bivariate Correlational Analyses were used to examine further the relationship between the age of first traumatic experience and Existential Well-Being Scores (Table 10) as well Religious Well-Being Scores (Table 11).

Bivariate Correlational Analyses between the age of first traumatic occurrence for each type of trauma and Existential Well-Being score revealed a significant positive correlation ($r = .58$, $p = .01$) between the "Age of First Illness" and Existential Well-Being scores as measured by the *Spiritual Well-Being Scale*. More specifically, as the age at the time of the first illness increased so did Existential Well-Being scores. Thus, the younger the participant was at the time of the trauma of illness, the lower the Existential Well-Being score. Additionally, a significant (r

= .81, p = .03) correlation was found between the "Age of First Completed Rape" and Existential Well-Being scores. More specifically, the younger the age at the time of the first completed rape, the lower the Existential Well-Being score. The data yielded no other significant correlations between the participant's age at the time of the remaining types of traumatic occurrences and Existential Well-Being scores.

Table 11

Relationship between Age of First Traumatic Occurrence and Existential Well-Being

Type of Trauma	(*N* =)	Pearson Correlation	Sig (2-tailed)
Age of First Witnessed Trauma	77	- .04	.764
Age of First Trauma from Accident	40	.10	.537
Age of First Trauma from Natural Disaster	22	- .12	.588
Age of First Trauma from Illness	18	.58*	.012*
Age of First Trauma from Physical Assault	92	.19	.067
Age of First Trauma from Attempted Rape	44	.05	.737
Age of First Trauma from Completed Rape	74	.81*	.028*
Age of First Trauma from Sexual Molestat.	55	- .11	.447
Age of First Trauma from Being Tormented	66	.18	.150
Age of First Causing Harm to Another	21	.36	.107

(Note: * Indicates significant results with p-value less than .05)

Bivariate Correlational Analyses between the age of first traumatic occurrence for each type of trauma and Religious Well-Being scores as measured by the *Spiritual Well-Being Scale* (Table 12). A significant positive correlation (r =. 28, p = .04) between "Age of First Trauma from Being Tormented/Stalked/Repeatedly Humiliated" and the Religious Well-Being score.

That is, the younger the participant's age at the time of first "Torment/Stalked/Repeatedly Humiliated" the lower the Religious Well-Being scores. Additionally, a significant positive correlation (r = .45, p = .04) was noted between "Age of Causing Harm to Another Person" and Religious Well-Being scores. This suggests that the younger the participant's age at the time of causing harm to another person, the lower their Religious Well- Being score. The data yielded no other significant correlations between the participant's age at the time of the remaining types of traumatic occurrences and Religious Well-Being scores.

Table: 12

Relationship between Age of First Traumatic Occurrence and Religious Well-Being

Type of Trauma	(*N* =)	Pearson Correlation	Sig (2-tailed)
Age of First Witnessed Trauma	77	-.11	.338
Age of First Trauma from Accident	40	.06	.710
Age of First Trauma from Natural Disaster	22	-.13	.543
Age of First Trauma from Illness	18	.29	.239
Age of First Trauma from Physical Assault	92	.20	.058
Age of First Trauma from Attempted Rape	44	.25	.104
Age of First Trauma from Completed Rape	74	.11	.362
Age of First Trauma from Sexual Molestat.	55	-.17	.227
Age of First Trauma from Being Tormented	66	.26*	.037*
Age of First Causing Harm to Another	21	.45*	.039*

(Note: * Indicates significant results with p-value less than .05)

Research Sub-question: (b) What is the relationship between the number of traumatic occurrences and the spiritual well-being of women with substance use disorders as measured by the Spiritual Well-Being Scale and the Trauma Assessment?

Bivariate Correlational analysis was used to explore the relationship between the number of traumatic occurrences from each type of trauma experienced by the participants and the spiritual well-being of women with substance use disorders. For each type of trauma, participants were asked how many times that trauma had occurred. Responses were added across all types of trauma to arrive at a total number of traumas. No significant relationship ($r = -.09$, $p = .336$) was found between the total number of traumatic occurrences and Spiritual Well-Being Scores (Table 13).

Table 13

Pearson correlation between Total Number of Traumatic Occurrences and Spiritual Well-Being

Spiritual Well Being	*(N=)*	*Pearson Correlation*	*Sig. (2-tailed)*
Number of Trauma Occurrences (*Total Trauma)*	108	-.09	.336

To further examine the impact of the number of traumatic occurrences on the Spiritual Well-Being scores for each type of trauma simultaneous (all ten predictor variables grouped together) multiple linear regression analysis was conducted to determine if Spiritual Well-Being scores could be predicted based on the number of traumas from each type of trauma experienced by the participants. The results of the simultaneous multiple linear regression with all ten predictor variables (type of trauma) included revealed no significant linear relationship between the number of traumas from each type of traumatic occurrence and Spiritual Well Being scores: $R^2 = .102$, $F(8, 99) = 1.41$, $p = .202$ (See Table 14).

Table 14

Summary of Multiple Regression for Number of Traumatic Occurrences and Spiritual Well-Being

Type of Trauma	B	SE(B)	β	*t*	Significance (2-tailed) (*N=108*)
Trauma Witnessed	1.69	1.24	.139	1.36	.175
Accident	2.45	1.94	.130	1.26	.211
Trauma Natural Disaster	2.42	2.78	.086	.896	.387
Trauma Phys. Assault	.27	1.51	.021	.181	.857
Attempted Rape	.56	1.69	.035	.329	.743
Completed Rape	-.42	1.45	-.031	-.287	.774
Sexual Molestation	-2.20	1.25	-.195	-1.75	.083
Being Tormented	-2.01	1.14	-.188	-1.76	.081

($R^2 = .10$)

Supplementary simultaneous (all ten predictor variables grouped together) multiple linear regression analyses were conducted to determine if Existential Well-Being scores could be predicted based on the number of traumas from each type of trauma experienced by the participants. The results of the simultaneous multiple linear regression with all ten predictor variables (type of trauma) included, revealed a significant negative relationship between the number of traumas from sexual molestation and the Existential Well-Being scores: $R^2 = .078$, $F(8, 99) = 1.04$, $p = -.045$. That is, as the number of traumas from sexual molestation increased the participant's existential well-being scores decreased (See Table 15).

Table 15

Summary of Multiple Regression for Number of Traumatic Occurrences and Existential Well-Being

Type of Trauma	B	SE(B)	*β*	*t*	Significance. (2-tailed) (*N* = *108*)
How Many Trauma Witnessed	- .03	.60	- .005	- .047	.963
How Many Trauma Accident	.88	.93	098	.938	.350
How Many Trauma Natural Disaster	1.35	1.33	.101	1.01	.316
How Many Trauma Phys. Assault	.77	.72	.124	1.07	.289
How Many Trauma from Attempted Rape	1.05	.81	.140	1.29	.199
How Many Trauma Completed Rape	-.20	.70	-.031	-.282	.779
How Many Trauma Sexual Molest.	-1.23	.60	- .229	-2.03	.045*
How Many Traumas Being Tormented/Stalked/Repeatedly Humiliated.	- .67	.55	-.133	- 1,23	.223

(R^2 = .078)

Supplementary simultaneous (all ten predictor variables grouped together) multiple linear regression analyses were conducted to determine if Religious Well-Being scores could be predicted based on the number of traumas from each type of trauma experienced by the participants. The results of the simultaneous multiple linear regression with all ten predictor variables (type of trauma) included, revealed a significant negative linear relationship between the number of witnessed traumas and the Religious Well-Being scores: R^2 =.14, F(8, 99) = 2.01, p = .026. That is, as the number of witnessed traumas increased the participant's religious well-being scores decreased (Table 16).

Table 16

Summary of Multiple Regression for Number of Traumatic Occurrences and Religious Well-Being

Type of Trauma	B	SE(B)	*β*	T	Sig. (2-tailed) (*N=108*)
How Many Trauma Witnessed	1.73	.763	.23	-2.26	.026*
How Many Trauma Accident	1.57	1.19	.13	1.32	.191
How Many Trauma Natural Disaster	1.07	1.71	.06	.627	.532
How Many Trauma Phys. Assault	- .50	.93	- .06	- .538	.592
How Many Trauma from Attempted Rape	- .49	1.04	- .05	- .475	.636
How Many Trauma Completed Rape	-.22	.89	-.03	-.248	.805
How Many Trauma Sexual Molestation	- .97	.77	-.14	-1.20	.211
How Many Trauma Being Tormented	-1.4	.70	-.20	-1.92	.058

(Note: R2 =.14)

Summary of Results

Three exploratory questions were addressed through statistical analysis: What is the relationship between type of trauma and spiritual well-being, in women with substance abuse disorders when comparing different types of trauma? What is the relationship between age of first traumatic occurrence and spiritual well-being in women with substance use disorders as measured by the *Spiritual Well-Being Scale* and the *Trauma Assessment*? What is the relationship between the number of traumatic occurrences and the spiritual well-being in women with substance use disorders as measured by the *Spiritual Well-Being Scale* and the *Trauma Assessment*?

For each of the ten types of trauma, an independent samples t-test was calculated to compare the mean Spiritual Well-Being score of those women who had experienced that type of trauma verses the mean Spiritual Well-Being score of those women who had not experienced that type of trauma. Of the ten types of trauma explored, there was a positive difference (p =. 047) between the mean Spiritual Well-Being scores among the women who reported the trauma of sexual molestation (mean = 90.4) and those who reported no history of sexual molestation (mean = 98.0). These results suggest that women with a reported history of sexual molestation yielded lower Spiritual Well-Being scores than women with no reported history of sexual molestation.

Bivariate correlation procedures indicated a positive association between age of first physical assault (r = .22, p = .039) and Spiritual Well-Being scores. Specifically, as the age of the first physical assault increased scores on the Spiritual Well-Being Scale also increased. Thus, the younger participants were at the age of their first physical assault, the lower their spiritual well-being score. A significant positive association (r = .24, p = .048) was also revealed between age of first trauma from being tormented/stalked/repeatedly humiliated and Spiritual Well-Being Scores. Specifically, as the younger the age at the time of first torment/stalked/repeatedly humiliated the lower the scores on the *Spiritual Well-Being Scale*. Additionally, there was significant positive association (r = .52, p = .016) between the age of first harm to another person and the participant's Spiritual Well-Being score. The younger the participant was when harm was caused to another person, the lower their Spiritual Well-Being score.

To examine the impact of the number of traumatic occurrences on the Spiritual Well-Being scores for each type of trauma, simultaneous (all ten predictor variables grouped together) multiple linear regression analysis was conducted to determine if Spiritual Well-Being scores,

Existential Well-Being sores and Religious Well-Being scores could be predicted based on the number of traumas experienced by the participants.

The results of the simultaneous multiple linear regression with all ten predictor variables (type of trauma) included revealed no significant linear relationship between the number of traumatic occurrences and Spiritual Well Being scores: $R^2 = .102$, $F(8, 99) = 1.41$, $p = .202$.

The results of the simultaneous multiple linear regression with all ten predictor variables (type of trauma) included revealed a significant negative relationship between the number of traumas from sexual molestation and Existential Well-Being scores: $R^2 = .078$, $F(8, 99) = 1.04$, $p = .045$. That is, as the number of traumas from sexual molestation increased the participant's existential well-being scores decreased.

The results of the simultaneous multiple linear regression with all ten predictor variables (type of trauma) included revealed a significant negative linear relationship between the number of witnessed traumas and the Religious Well-Being scores: $R^2 = .140$, $F(8, 99) = 2.01$, $p = .026$. That is, as the number of witnessed traumas increased the participant's religious well-being scores decreased.

Chapter Summary

This chapter covered the sampling procedures, data preparation, descriptive statistics, and statistical procedures of the research study. The statistical procedures included independent samples t-tests, bivariate correlational analysis, and simultaneous multiple regression. The chapter concluded with a summary of results. The next chapter will discuss findings in relation to the literature, the strengths and limitations of the research and future research findings in relation to the literature, the strengths and limitations of the research, and possible directions for future research.

CHAPTER FIVE

DISCUSSION

Introduction to the Chapter

In this chapter, a summary of the results is presented and interpreted in light of current literature. A review of the theoretical constructs underlying the methodology and sample selection is discussed. Results of data collection and statistical processing for each research question are provided. Limitations of the study are presented and recommendations and implications for future research in counselor education for rehabilitation and addictions fields are offered.

Summary of the Study

Concise Review of the Study

This study explored the relationship between trauma and spiritual well-being of 108 women with substance use disorders. Multiple regression, correlational analysis, and independent sample t-tests analysis provided a descriptive profile of the participants and allowed examination of the relationship between trauma and spiritual well-being. Specifically, the study explored the relationship between type of trauma occurrence, age of first trauma occurrence, frequency of trauma occurrences and participants' level of spiritual well-being.

Theoretical constructs investigate. Fowler's (1981) theory of faith development provided the theoretical framework for this research. Fowler's (1981) theory offers a comprehensive lifespan perspective of spiritual development. Fowler contends that stages of faith development reveal important distinctions in the level of complexity with which individuals understand self, the values and commitments that guide them, their relationship with others, and their relationship to the divine (Cartwright, 2001). According to Fowler (1981), life crisis often impedes or arrests faith development and sense of spiritual well-being.

A review of the literature from Chapter Two established the prevalence of trauma experiences for women with substance use disorders (Najavitis, 2002; Najavitis, Weiss, & Shaw, 1997; Tuchman, 2010). Further, the review of the literature outlined the mitigating elements of spirituality in the recovery of co-occurring trauma and substance use disorders (Vis &Boynton, 2008). The current study addresses paucity in the literature concerning the relationship between trauma and the spiritual well-being for women with substance use disorders. Specifically, the relationship between type of trauma occurrence, age of first trauma occurrence, and frequency of trauma occurrence on the overall spiritual well-being of women with substance use disorders.

Participants and data collection. As reported through the literature review in Chapter Two and the discussion of methodology in Chapter three, this study utilized archival data collected from a comprehensive gender inclusive study examining the impact of Trauma on the Spiritual Development of Individuals with Substance Use disorders. The initial study contained males and females enrolled in a comprehensive, multi-year, modified therapeutic community (TC), who met DSM IV-R diagnostic criteria for a substance use disorder. The present study reflects gender specific data obtained from 108 female participants with an identified a history of trauma and a diagnosed substance use disorder. Between April 2010 and August 2012, each participant completed three self-report questionnaires: *Supplemental Demographic Information* form (See Appendix A), *Adapted Trauma Assessment* (See Appendix B), and *Spiritual Well-Being Scale* (See Appendix C). The questionnaires were completed in a single session lasting up to 90 minutes. Additional demographic information was obtained from the agency database.

During this time, 115 participants completed the questionnaires. Of these, 108 participants had no missing data. Therefore, they constituted the study sample.

Discussion

Review of the Results

The results reflect descriptive data (demographic and frequency data) as well as outcome data from the *Adapted Trauma Assessment* (Appendix B) and *Spiritual Well-Being Scale* (Appendix C). Data collection instruments and the results of statistical procedures were compared to related literature. Multiple regression, correlational analysis, and independent sample t-test procedures were the statistical analyses performed to test the research questions. An alpha level of .05 was used when analyzing the data.

Descriptive Data and Past Research

Descriptive data includes age, racial/ethnical group, years of education, age at first alcohol use, age of first drug (other than alcohol) use, *Adapted Trauma Assessment* data, and *Spiritual Well-Being* scores. Variables were compared to similar research concerning the role of spirituality in the recovery of women with co-occurring trauma and substance use disorders.

Gender and age. As previously noted, the present study was single-site, gender specific study. The sample contained 108 adult females. Historically, single-site, quantitative, gender-specific research studies of women with co-occurring trauma and substance use disorders are infrequent and when available, yield smaller sample sizes than the current study.

For example, Covington, et al. (2008) examined the impact of gender-specific/trauma informed treatment for adult women at a single-site, social learning, residential program similar to a therapeutic community (TC). Although a sample of one hundred ninety-five (n = 195) was noted at the completion of the 45-day orientation and stabilization period, only eighty-four participants (n = 84) remained at the study's end. A noted exception was Fullilove's et al. (1993) study of violence, trauma, and PTSD among women with substance use disorders (n = 109).

To achieve larger samples, gender specific studies for women tend to employ multi-site participation. Cocozza, et. al, (2005) completed a nine-site, mixed milieu (inpatient and outpatient) study with a sample size of two thousand twenty-six (n = 2026), and Hein, et al. (2010) completed a seven-site, outpatient study with a sample size of three hundred-fifty-three (n = 353).

Age. The current study yielded a mean age of 38. This is consistent with mean ages from the Covington, et al. (2008), Cocozza, et al. (2005), and Hein, et al. (2010), whose studies contained a mean ages of 30, 32, and 39 years respectively. However, the demographics for the current research are not representative of all females because only adults were surveyed.

Racial/ethnic groups. In the current study, 54 (50%) of the participants identified as White/Caucasian, 52 (48%), as Black/African American, and 2 (1.9%) as American Indian/Alaska Native. No participants identified as Asian, Hispanic/Latina, or Native Hawaiian/Pacific Islander. Thus, White/Caucasian and Black/African Americans are the most represented, with markedly low or no representation from Hispanic/Latina, Native American/Alaskan Natives, and Native Hawaiian/Pacific Islanders.

The racial/ethnic data collected for the current study is similar to other gender specific studies in that White/Caucasian and Black/African American participants are represented more frequently than other ethnic groups. Cocozza's, et al., (2005) sample was 50% White/Caucasian, 25% Black/African American, 17% Hispanic/Latina, and 7% were classified as "other". Hein's et al. (2010) sample was 46% White/Caucasian, 34% Black/African American, 7%

Hispanic/Latina and .6 % were classified as "other". Likewise, Wiechelt's et al. (2011) sample was 46% Black/African American, 41% White/Caucasian and 14% were classified as "other".

Education. Participants were asked to identify the number of years of education they had completed. Participant education ranged from 8 to 16 years, with a mean of 11.78, a median of 12, and a standard deviation of 1.2 years. Thus, the typical participant had a high school education/GED. This level of education is consistent with previous studies (Cocozza, et al., 2005; Covington, et al., 2008; Hein, et. al., 2010; Wiechelt, et al., (2011); Fullilove, et al., 1993).

Substance Use. Participants were asked to identify the age of first alcohol use, first drug (other than alcohol) use, and primary drug of choice. One hundred-seven (107) of the 108 participants reported a history of alcohol use with the age of first use ranging from 4 to 24 years, a mean of 13.1 years, a median of 14.0 years, and a standard deviation of 4.6 years. Thus the typical participant began using alcohol between the age of 13 and 14. This suggests that the typical age of first alcohol use occurred when the participant was in the 7th or 8th grade if typical educational progression occurred. In research conducted by the National Institute of Health (2006), the age of first alcohol use was approximately 14 years of age. This finding is consistent with age of first use for the women in the current study.

One hundred-six (106) of the 108 participants identified a history of drug (other than alcohol) use. Age of first drug use ranged from 9 to 24 years, with a mean of 16 years, median of 15.0 years, and a standard deviation of 3.52 years. Thus, the typical participant initiated drug (other than alcohol) use during her high school years. The National Survey on Drug Use and Health (2012) revealed that while the majority of women initiate the use of drugs (other than alcohol) around the age of 18, approximately 14% commence drug use prior to 13 years of age. These findings are fairly consistent with the data obtained from the current study.

Participants were asked to identify their primary drug of choice. Primary substance of use for the current study was cocaine (n = 44, 40.7%), alcohol (n = 27, 25%), opiates (n = 26, 24%), marijuana (n = 6, 6%), and methamphetamines (n = 4, 4%). Thus, the most frequently identified drug of choice was cocaine. The prevalence of cocaine and alcohol use for substance abusing women was consistent with past studies (Covington, et al., 2008; Cocozza, et al., 2005; Hein, et al., 2010; Fullilove, et al., 1998).

Data Collection Instruments and Past Research

In addition to demographic identifiers, this study utilized a researcher *Adapted Trauma Assessment* (Appendix B) and *Spiritual Well-Being Scale* (Appendix C).

Type of Trauma. Participants for this study were asked to identify type(s) of trauma(s) experienced. The most represented to least represented type of trauma was completed rapes (n = 74, 69%); physical assault (n = 73, 68%); being tormented, stalked or repeatedly humiliated (n = 66, 61%); causing harm to another person (n = 63, 58%); witnessing a traumatic event (n = 61, 56%); sexual molestation (n = 55, 51%); attempted rapes (n = 44, 41%); accidents (n = 40, 37%); natural disaster (n = 22, 20%); illness (n = 18, 17%), and combat (n = 0). Thus, non-violent trauma(s) (traumas resulting from accidents and natural disasters) were reported less frequently than violent traumas (traumas resulting from intentional violent physical and/or sexual victimization of an innocent person).

Prevalence rates of traumatic occurrences among women with substance use disorders found in this study are consistent with studies by Covington (2007), Najavitis (2004), Taylor, (2010), and Weichelt (2008) that identify traumatic occurrences among women with substance use disorders range from 55% to 95%. These findings are also congruous to reports by the Center for Disease Control and Prevention (CDC, 2005) that one in five women report a history of completed rape, one in six women report a history of being stalked, and one in three women report a history of physical violence by an intimate partner.

Furthermore, variation in prevalence rates between non-violent traumatic occurrences and violent traumatic occurrences in this study are consistent with the findings of Kennedy et al. (2004) that suggest that non-violent traumatic occurrences differ in intensity, scope, and frequency from violent traumatic occurrences.

Age at First Trauma. The age of first traumatic occurrence for the current study ranged from 2 to 34 years, with a mean of 10 years, a median of 9.50 years. The histogram (Figure 2) showed a slight positive skew (1.1), indicating that the majority of participants experienced their first trauma at younger rather than older ages.

These findings indicate that the majority of participants experienced their first trauma at younger rather than older ages are consistent with the findings of Enlow et al., (2013), Finkelhor et al. (1990), and Taylor (2010). Enlow et al. (2013) found that between birth and age six, 38% of children had witnessed interpersonal trauma (physical violence toward mother by her partner in the home) with 28% experiencing co-occurring witnessed trauma and experienced maltreatment. Among those experiencing maltreatment, 49% were physically abused, 54 % reported emotional abuse (constant harassment or berating, chronically finding fault and harsh criticism), 48% emotionally neglected (emotionally unresponsive parent or neglect of physical needs), and 18% were sexually abused (genital contact between the child and a person at least five years or older). Similarly, reports offered by the CDC (2005) suggest that one in four women will be sexually abused before age eighteen. Of those, 10% will be sexually abused between birth and three years of age, 28.4% will experience sexual abuse between four and seven years of age, and 25% will experience sexual abuse between eight and eleven years of age.

Number of Trauma Occurrences. The number of trauma occurrences in the current study ranged from 1 to 26 occurrences, with a mean of 11.2 and a median of 11.5 occurrences. The histogram (Figure 1) showed a fairly normal distribution. Approximately 2/3 of the subjects reported experiencing between five and seventeen trauma occurrences. The prevalence of multiple forms of trauma among women, specifically those with substance abuse disorders has been supported by Enlow et al. (2013) and Najavitis (2002) and Covington (2007). According to Gordon (2002), the bi-directional nature of trauma and addiction predisposes women to greater risks of recurring trauma. According to the CDC (2010) women with a prior history of sexual victimization are more than 100% more likely to be re-victimized.

Classification of Offender. Participants were asked to classify the offender for each type and incidence of trauma. Categories of offenders included: family member (other than partner or spouse), friend/acquaintance, partner/spouse and stranger. Classification for the offender at the age of the first occurrence of each type of trauma is shown in Table 4. The data suggests that the partner/spouse is the most frequently reported offender for the first traumatic occurrences of witnessed trauma, physical assault, trauma from being tormented, stalked, or repeatedly humiliated, and cause of harm to another person. Family member was the most frequently reported offender for the first traumatic occurrence of sexual molestation. Friend/Acquaintance was the most frequently reported offender for the first traumatic occurrence of attempted and completed rape.

The classification of offender for the identified types of trauma occurrences in this study are consistent with those found by the American Psychological Association (APA, 20014), Center for Disease Control and Prevention (2010), National Institute of Justice (2010), Taylor (2010) and Wiechelt, (2008).

Taylor (2010), and Wiechelt, (2008) found that violence initiated by a partner/spouse is the most frequently reported (57% to 85%) first traumatic occurrence for "Witnessed Trauma", "Trauma from Physical Assault", "Trauma from being Tormented, Stalked, or Repeatedly Humiliated", and "Cause of Harm to Another Person. The CDC (2005, 2010) corroborates the findings of Taylor (2010) and Wiechelt (2008). However, their findings indicate that sexual assault is present in fifty percent (50%) of the women who report intimate partner/spouse physical assault.

Findings of this study regarding friend/acquaintance as the most frequently reported offender for the first traumatic occurrence of "Attempted Rape", and "Completed Rape" were supported by findings of the CDC (2010), and the National Institute of Justice (2010). According to the CDC (2010) the identified perpetrator in forty percent (40%) of reported sexual abuse cases among women is an acquaintance. Thirteen percent (13%) of the perpetrators were identified as a stranger. Similarly, the National Institute of Justice (2010) found that eight (8) out of ten (10) women who report being sexually assaulted identified an acquaintance as the attacker.

However, findings in this study that a family member is the perpetrator of the first trauma of "Sexual Molestation" among women are inconsistent with the findings of the American Psychological Association (APA, 2014). In their findings the APA (2014) reported that thirty percent (30%) of perpetrators of sexual trauma among women are a family member whereas sixty percent (60%) of perpetrators are a non-family member (friends, babysitter, childcare worker, neighbor), and ten percent (10%) are classified as a stranger. Differences in findings between this study and those of the American Psychological Association (2014) could be attributed to variations in the sample size and sample population (type and level of substance abuse and/mental health treatment involvement, ethnicity of participants, age of the participants, substance use history).

Spiritual Well-Being Scale Scores

Ellison's (1983) *Spiritual Well-Being Scale* (Appendix C) is a self-report questionnaire containing 20 questions. The questions are rated on a 6-point Likert scale ranging from 1 (strongly agree) to 6 (strongly disagree), with higher totals representing greater spiritual well-being.

The *Spiritual Well-Being Scale* generates an existential well-being score (EWB), a religious well-being score (RWB), and an overall or total Spiritual Well-Being Score (SWB). Existential Well-Being scores range from 20-60, with higher scores suggesting greater levels of existential well-being (level of life perspective and sense of meaning and purpose. Religious Well-Being scores range from 10 to 60, with higher scores suggesting greater levels of religious and existential well-being (how participants view their relationship, sense of satisfaction, and connectedness with God or the divine). The Spiritual Well-Being score (SWB) is a composite of the RWB and EWB scores. The Spiritual Well-Being score provides a measure of the participant's overall spiritual well-being. Scores can range from 40 to 120.

The Spiritual Well-Being Scale has been used with a variety of groups. Scores presented in comparison to the current sample include: (a) religious groups, (b) graduate students, (c) psychiatric patients, (d) criminal justice inmates, (e) substance abuse clients, (f) Alcoholic Anonymous members and (g) women with HIV.

In the current study, Existential Well-Being (EWB) scores ranged from 20 to 60, with a mean of 46.7, a median of 47.0, and a standard deviation of 9.4. These scores are similar to women being treated for HIV (46.6, SD = 9.0) and are higher than those for males and females receiving outpatient psychiatric services (39.5, SD = 10.5); having one to three years of Alcoholic Anonymous involvement (43.8 SD = 15.4); females having histories of sexual abuse (39.3); female graduate students reporting a history of traumatic experiences with no identified religious orientation (41.6, SD = 9.4); and criminal justice inmates reporting no history religious involvement (40.7, SD = 9.20; Bonet, 2009; Bufford, Paloutzian, & Ellison, 1991; Granucci, 1994). However, the E WB scores in this study are lower than individuals (pastors and seminarians) reporting an affiliation with religious organizations (49.5, SD = 5.5); graduate students reporting a religious orientation (49.5, SD = 5.5); criminal justice inmates reporting a history of religious involvement (50.1, 10.4); and individuals having a SUD at six month post-inpatient and outpatient treatment (48.9, SD = 15.9; Bufford, et al., 1991; NIH, 2009; Steele, 1999).

Religious Well-Being (RWB) scores ranged from 10 to 60, with a mean of 47.4, a median of 50.5, and a standard deviation of 12.46. These scores are similar to the RWB scores for males and females receiving outpatient psychiatric services (46.5, SD = 15.94); females reporting a history of sexual abuse (46.5, SD = 11.5); female graduate students reporting a history of traumatic experiences with an identified religious orientation (53.6, SD = 6.3); and criminal justice inmates reporting a history of religious involvement (51, SD = 10.4; Bufford, et al., 1991; Granucci, 1994; NIH, 2009; Steele, 1999).

Religious Well-Being scores in this study were higher than those receiving outpatient psychiatric services (males and females; 39.5, SD = 8.9) and female graduate students reporting a history of traumatic experiences with no identified religious orientation (29.7, SD = 15.9; Bonet, 2009; Bufford, et al., 1991; Granucci, 1994). However, the current RWB scores are lower than individuals (pastors and seminarians) reporting an affiliation with religious organizations

(58, SD = 6.3); males and females reporting one to three years of sobriety through Alcoholics Anonymous involvement (45, SD = 10.5; females treated for HIV (51.9, SD = 7.8); and criminal justice inmates who report a history of religious involvement (51, SD = 10.4); and criminal justice inmates reporting a no religious involvement (35.6, SD = 9.2; Bufford, et al., 1991; NIH, 2009; Steele, 1999).

Spiritual Well-Being (SWB) scores ranged from 40 to 120 with a mean of 94, a median of 98.5, and a standard deviation of 19.86. These scores are consistent with the SWB scores of females reporting a history of sexual abuse (93.3, SD = 11.5) and females being treated for HIV (94.4, SD = 10.4; Bufford, et al., 1991; NIH, 2009; Steel, 1999).

Spiritual Well-Being Scores in this study were higher than those for males and females receiving outpatient psychiatric services (85.8, SD = 19.6; males and females reporting one to three years of sobriety through Alcoholics Anonymous involvement (83.8; SD = 15.3); and female graduate students reporting a history of traumatic experiences with no religious orientation (73.6, SD = 16.3; Bonet, 2009; Bufford, et al., 1991; Granucci, 1994).

However, the SWB scores for this study are lower than scores for individuals reporting an affiliation with religious organizations (104.3, SD = 9.5); female graduate students reporting a history of traumatic experiences with an identified religious orientation (70.4, SD = 17.9); criminal justice inmates reporting a history of religious involvement (105, SD = 13.5); and males and females with a SUD reporting six month post-inpatient and outpatient treatment sobriety (100.4, SD = 15.9; Bufford, et al., 1991; Steele, 1999).

Several observations can be made from the current study's scores and the comparison sample scores. First, scores for individuals reporting spiritual orientation or affiliation with religious organizations tend to be higher. Second, scores support a connection between spiritual well-being and other dimensions of well-being including recovery from illness, addressing psychiatric symptomatology, maintaining recovery form SUDs, and coping with incarceration. Third, involvement in a supportive treatment and community supports contributes to higher levels of existential and religious well-being. Fourth, the *Spiritual Well-Being Scale* is a useful instrument for evaluating fluctuations in spiritual well-being over time and in relationship to traumatic life events. Specifically, for those with low spiritual well-being scores who may be experiencing spiritual distress. This is in keeping with Fowler's (1983) belief that spiritual development fluctuates and changes over the course of one's lifespan (Fowler, 1983).

With regard to Fowler's model of faith development, the women's scores in the current study suggest that they are able to engage with others and with the divine to formulate a spiritual identity that permits integration of their internal and external experiences. These women exhibit social perspective taking and cognitively embrace a broader understanding of shared interpersonal perspectives regarding spirituality. Thus their ability to benefit from the relational aspects of the treatment experience broadens. For example, a woman with co-occurring disorders can individualize 12-step recovery principles and benefit from experiences and perspectives of others often found in community and treatment groups. This individualized integration provides a supportive framework for examination and reorganization of their previously held system of spiritual beliefs, symbols, values, relationships, and commitments. When this exploration is encouraged in a clinical or supportive group setting, assimilative spiritual autonomy develops. Women with the scores identified in this study demonstrate an increased ability to adapt to paradoxical complexities of faith and spirituality. This spiritual growth fosters an understanding of the universality and mutuality of the spiritual process where women can personalize their commitment to, and understanding of recovery principles, yet it promotes a sense of shared meaning and purpose with those around them.

Furthermore, the SWB scores in this study are consistent with those identified by Fallot and Heckman (2005) which showed higher SWB scores for women with co-occurring trauma and substance use disorders. Both the current findings and Fallot and Heckman (2005) findings suggest that spirituality has a role in supporting posttraumatic growth and resiliency of women with co-occurring disorders.

Profile of the Sample

The variables of this study provide a representative profile of the women in this sample. The majority of the women in this sample were White/Caucasian and Black/African American women in their late thirties. Most had obtained a high school education or equivalent. The typical participant initiated alcohol use between the age of 13 and 14, and drug use (other then alcohol) around the age of 16. Cocaine was identified as the primary substance used. The majority of the participants reported experiencing eleven traumatic occurrences. Most had experienced their first trauma between 9 and 10 years of age. "Physical Assault" and "Completed Rapes" were the most frequently reported type of trauma occurrence. The mean Spiritual Well-Being Score (94.0) indicated the majority of the participants had scores representative of those who are developmental process spiritual complexities in a manner that fosters posttraumatic growth.

The profile for this sample underscores complex and co-occurring clinical concerns of women with substance use disorders. Incorporation of comprehensive, gender-specific, trauma-informed, and trauma-specific service delivery and clinical practice recognizes the unique life experiences of women including the prevalence of co-occurring trauma and substance use disorders and the impact of those events on treatment presentation, symptomology, retention and completion (Covington et al., 2008). The incorporation of spirituality in the provision of care expands the scope of intrinsic and extrinsic supports that provide mitigating factors in trauma recovery.

Research Findings.

Research Question: What is the relationship between type of trauma and spiritual well-being, in women with substance abuse disorders when comparing different types of trauma?

For each type of trauma, an independent samples t-test was calculated to compare the Spiritual Well-Being Score (SWB) of women who had experienced that type of trauma versus the mean Spiritual Well-Being Score (SWB) of those women who had not experienced that type of trauma. The only type of trauma for which there was a significant difference was Sexual Molestation ($p = .047$). Women who reported experiencing the trauma of "Sexual Molestation" had a significantly lower Spiritual Well-Being score than those who had not experienced the trauma of "Sexual Molestation".

To further examine the impact of type of trauma on the Spiritual Well-Being score (SWB), a simultaneous (all ten predictor variables grouped together) multiple linear regression analysis was conducted to determine if spiritual well-being scores could be predicted based on the nature of the trauma experienced by the participants. The results of the simultaneous multiple linear regressions with all ten predictor variables (type of trauma) included, revealed no significant relationship between type of trauma and Spiritual Well-Being scores.

The findings of the Independent Samples t-test are in keeping with previous studies that demonstrated a decrease in spiritual well-being among women with histories of sexually based traumas including sexual molestation (Doehring, 1993; Kennedy Davis & Taylor, 1998; Pritt, 1998; Ryan, 1998).

Research indicates that sexual molestation for women often occurs at earlier rather than later ages (Enlow et al., 2013; Finkelhor et al. 1990; and Taylor, 2010). With regard to the spiritual development for women with a reported history of childhood sexual molestation, Fowler's (1983) model of faith development offers insight into the potential impact of childhood trauma on spiritual growth and development. According to Fowler (1983), children typically exhibit characteristics found in the pre-stage, birth to three years of age (undifferentiated faith), stage one, age three to six or seven (intuitive-projective faith) and stage two, age seven to elven or twelve (mythic-literal faith). It is in the pre-stage of Fowler's model of faith development that basic forms of trust are established. Fowler contends that all that comes later is built on this basis of trust or mistrust. Children in stage one and two demonstrate significant dependence on perceptions of authority figures. Children can be powerfully and permanently influenced by examples, moods, actions, and stories represented in the visible faith of the primary adults in their life (Fowler, 1981). Children in stage one and two lack the ability to fully process and interpret complex and often confounding concepts and experiences (Fowler, 1983). Trauma occurrences experienced in childhood, specifically those perpetrated by a parent or parental figure, can create distorted images of the divine that form the framework for either benevolent or punitive spiritual or religious ideologies.

Research Findings sub-question A: What is the relationship between age of first traumatic occurrence and spiritual well-being in women with substance use disorders as measured by the *Spiritual Well-Being Scale* and the *Trauma Assessment*?

Bi-variate correlational analyses were used to explore the nature of the relationship between the age of first traumatic occurrence and Spiritual Well-Being scores. The results indicated a significant correlation between age of first trauma from "Physical Assault" (r =.178, p = .039), "Being Tormented, Stalked, or Repeatedly Humiliated" (r = .244, p= .048), "Causing Harm" to another person (r = .519, p = .016) and Spiritual Well-Being scores. For each of these types of trauma as the age at first physical assault increases so did Spiritual Well-Being scores. Thus, the younger the participant was at the age of each of these traumas, the lower her spiritual well-being scores.

Supplementary Bivariate Correlational Analyses were used to further examine the relationship between the age of first traumatic experience and Existential Well-Being Scores as well Religious Well-Being Scores.

Bivariate Correlational Analyses between the age of first traumatic occurrence for each type of trauma and Existential Well-Being score revealed a significant positive correlation (r = .575, p = .012) between the "Age of First Illness" as well as "Age of First Completed Rape" (r = .811, p = .028) and Existential Well-Being scores as measured by the *Spiritual Well-Being Scale*. More specifically, as the age at the time of these traumas increased so did Existential Well-Being scores. Thus, the younger the participant was at the time the trauma of "Illness" and "Completed Rape" occurred, the lower the Existential Well-Being score.

Bivariate Correlational Analyses between the age of first traumatic occurrence for each type of trauma and Religious Well-Being scores revealed a significant positive correlation (r =. 275, p = .037) between "Age of First Trauma from Being Tormented/Stalked/Repeatedly Humiliated" and age at the time of "Causing Harm" to another person (r =. 453, p = .039) and Religious Well-Being scores. Thus, the younger the participant's age at the time trauma from being "Tormented/Stalked/Repeatedly Humiliated" and of "Causing Harm" to another person, the lower their Religious Well- Being score.

These findings regarding the age of first trauma and Spiritual Well-Being scores are consistent with those of Fallott and Heckman (2005) who found that sexually based traumas experienced in childhood resulted in lower levels of spiritual well-being, diminished capacities for meaning making (intrinsic well-being), decreased participation in religious practices, more expressed anger at God (religious well-being), and relational distancing from others (extrinsic well-being).

Briggs-Gowan, Carter, and Ford (2012) and Masters and Curtis, (2000) support the cycle of violence model that suggests that individuals who experience harm (physical, sexual, and emotional) often become perpetrators of violence toward others . Briggs-Gowan, Carter, and Ford (2012) and Masters and Curtis, (2000) suggest that prior forms of adaptation become hierarchically integrated into later patterns of self-defeating and self-destructive behavioral and emotional adaptations. They contend that adversative patterns interfere with developmental milestones hinder the ability to access and implement internal and external resources to successfully negotiate developmentally salient issues. Thus, victims of violence and maltreatment display patterns of violence and maltreatment to others.

Research Findings sub-question B: What is the relationship between the number of traumatic occurrences and the spiritual well-being in women with substance use disorders as measured by the *Spiritual Well-Being Scale* and the *Trauma Assessment*?

Bivariate Correlational analysis was used to explore the relationship between the number of traumatic occurrences and the spiritual well-being of women with substance use disorders. For each type of trauma, participants were asked how many times each type of trauma had occurred. Responses were added across all types of trauma to arrive at a total number of traumas. No significant relationship (r = - .093, p =. 34) was found between the total number of traumatic occurrences and Spiritual Well-Being Scores.

To further examine the impact of the number of traumatic occurrences on the Spiritual Well-Being scores for each type of trauma, simultaneous (all ten predictor variables grouped together) multiple regression analysis was conducted to determine if Spiritual Well-Being scores, could be predicted based on the number of traumas experienced by the participants. The results of the simultaneous multiple linear regressions with all ten predictor variables (type of trauma) included, revealed no significant relationship between the number of traumatic occurrences and Spiritual Well Being scores.

Supplementary simultaneous (all ten predictor variables grouped together) multiple linear regression analyses were conducted to determine if Existential and Religious Well-Being scores could be predicted based on the number of traumas experienced by the participants. The results of the simultaneous multiple linear regressions with all ten predictor variables (type of trauma) included, revealed a significant negative relationship between the number of traumas from sexual molestation and the Existential Well-Being scores. That is, as the number of traumas from sexual molestation increased the participant's existential well-being scores decreased. A significant negative relationship was revealed between the number of "Witnessed Traumas" and the Religious Well-Being scores. That is, as the number of witnessed traumas increased the participant's religious well-being scores decreased.

The findings regarding Existential Well-Being and Religious Well-Being are consistent with those of Fallot and Heckman's (2005) study on women, co-occurring disorders that revealed lower levels of existential and religious coping and well-being. However, they are inconsistent with their findings regarding overall Spiritual Well-Being. According to Fallot and Heckman

(2005), more frequent childhood physical abuse and sexual violence are associated with lower overall levels spiritual coping and spiritual well-being. The findings of the current study support those Doehring (1993), who found that women with frequent trauma occurrences in early childhood had a negative image of God. However, he found that women who had positive religious experiences as children were more likely to have a greater image of the divine and a higher level of spiritual well-being.

Additionally, evidence suggests that the experience of multiple types of traumatic occurrences (violent and non-violent) reinforces a cumulative impact on post-trauma symptom risk (Graham-Bermann, et al., 2012).

Summary of Analyses and Findings

Three research questions were addressed through statistical analysis:

What is the relationship between type of trauma and spiritual well-being, in women with substance abuse when disorders when comparing different types of trauma?

Sub-question: (a) *Research Findings sub-question A:* What is the relationship between age of first traumatic occurrence and spiritual well-being in women with substance use disorders as measured by the *Spiritual Well-Being Scale* and the *Trauma Assessment*?

Sub-question: (b) *Research Findings sub-question B:* What is the relationship between the number of traumatic occurrences and the spiritual well-being in women with substance use disorders as measured by the *Spiritual Well-Being Scale* and the *Trauma Assessment*?

When addressing the type of trauma and spiritual well-being for each type of trauma, an independent samples t-test was calculated to compare the Spiritual Well-Being Score (SWB) of those women who had experienced that type of trauma versus the mean Spiritual Well-Being

Score (SWB) of those women who had not experienced that type of trauma. Women who reported experiencing sexual molestation had a significantly lower Spiritual Well-Being score than those who had not.

Addressing the Age of first trauma and spiritual well-being, bivariate correlational analyses were used to explore the nature of the relationship between the age of first traumatic occurrence and Spiritual Well-Being scores. The results indicated a significant positive correlation between age of first traumas from "Physical Assault", "Being Tormented, Stalked, or Repeatedly Humiliated", "Causing Harm" to another person and Spiritual Well-Being scores. For each of these types of trauma as the age at first occurrence increases so did Spiritual Well-Being scores. Thus, the younger the participant was at the age of each of these trauma occurrences, the lower her spiritual well-being scores.

Bivariate Correlational analysis as well as simultaneous (all ten predictor variables grouped together) Multiple Linear Regression analysis were conducted to explore the nature of the relationship between the number of traumatic occurrences and Spiritual Well-Being scores. No significant relationship was found between the total number of traumatic occurrences and Spiritual Well-Being Scores.

Limitations of the study

According to Neuman (2006), research studies have both strengths and limitations that impact the quality of the results. Although this study was conducted in an appropriate and skillful way, it is essential to recognize the limitations. Limitations of this study include research design, sampling, and instrumentation.

Research design

The current study utilized a correlational rather than an experimental research design. Thus, a causal relationship cannot be assumed (Gall, Borg & Gall, 1986). A correlational research design explores the nature of the relationship(s) and the measure of relationship(s) between the variables. Even when significant correlations were found between variables, the relationship may be better explained by an extraneous variable(s) not measured in the study. For this research, level of spiritual well-being prior to entering treatment, prior treatment interventions, length of treatment involvement, and external support systems are potential peripheral influences that could impact the research findings.

Archival data collection was used for this study. The primary advantage for using archival data was the flexibility it offered when examining information collected over a 24-month period that included individuals at various stages of program involvement. The primary disadvantage is the inability to gather missing data from participants. For example, missing data lowered the current sample from 115 to 108. An additional limitation for the use of archival data is that the data reflects the response in that given point in time. The data does not address changes over time.

Sampling Limitations

Participant selection for this study used a selective sampling method, where participants were deliberately chosen based on relevant characteristics (Heppner et al., 2008). Eligible participants were limited to adult female residents of a two-year modified therapeutic community with a diagnosed substance use disorder and a history of at least on traumatic occurrence. The findings may not be representative of women different treatment milieus.

Although data was obtained from individuals who had resided in various geographical regions within the United States prior to entering treatment, the current research was not able to verify the geographic origins of its participants. There may have been geographic trends within the United States that were not addressed in instrumentation. Such geographic variance may explain differences among respondent's answers regarding spirituality and spiritual well-being.

Additionally, sampling was limited with regard to a sample of convenience. Use of a single-site sampling method yielded a relatively small sample size (n=108) as compared to multiple-site gender specific studies. This study also utilized a non-fixed protocol inclusive of participants at various stages of program involvement with varying trauma experiences and varying degrees of treatment intervention. External influences may impact individual attitudes and behaviors such that determining whether changes in individuals' spiritual well-being are due to traumatic events or treatment intervention may be impossible.

The lack of ethnic diversity in the sample is also a limitation. The ethnic composition of the sample was predominately Caucasian and African-American. Limitations in the cultural and ethnic diversity of the participants necessitate the use of caution when generalizing the results to other ethnic groups.

Instrumentation Limitations

This study utilized data from the agency data base and the *Supplemental Demographic Form*. Sample demographics included age, ethnicity, number of years of education, age of first alcohol use, age of first drug (other than alcohol) use, and legal history. The demographic data provided a useful description of the sample. However, as previously noted, demographic factors not included in this study may influence the research findings. Additionally, demographic factors related to living situation prior to entering treatment, family support, marital status, and prior treatment intervention have been found to influence overall well-being (Kaplan, 2008; Laudet & White, 2010). Future research, which includes these factors, may provide additional information concerning trauma and spirituality.

The use of self-report measures (*Spiritual Well-Being Scale* and *Adapted Trauma Assessment*) is subject to participant bias, which is the tendency of the participant to respond in the way they think the evaluator wants them to respond. As a result the findings may not be an accurate reflection or representation of the information (Van Ryn & Vinokur, 1992).

Trauma related variables for this study were measured by a researcher adapted version of the *Traumatic Life Events Questionnaire* (Elhai, Gray, Kashdan, & Franklin, 2005). The *Adapted Trauma Assessment* (Appendix C), in keeping with the TLEQ, was a comprehensive measure that assessed exposure to multiple forms of potentially traumatic events consistent with *Diagnostic and Statistical Manual IV* posttraumatic stress disorder criterion A-1. While the *Adapted Trauma Assessment* expanded the data in a manner that permits comparison of the types of trauma occurrence, frequency of trauma occurrence, and age of occurrence consistent with the stated research questions, generalizability with studies using the TLEQ may be limited.

Despite these limitations, the study has conceptual and methodological strengths. This study is one of the few to examine type of trauma, age of first trauma occurrence, and frequency of trauma occurrence on the subjective spiritual well-being of women with substance use disorders. Due to the scarcity of research in this area, the methods of this study were appropriate and allowed for the examination of multiple variables. Agency support of the conceptual ideas of the study and involvement in coordination of study participation promoted evidenced-based practice, reducing the harmful effects of the research-practice schism noted in literature (Davis, 2006).

Implications for Rehabilitation and Addiction Administrators, and Counselors.

Integration of comprehensive gender-responsive, trauma-informed, and trauma-specific care necessitates organizational structures and service delivery systems that understand the multidimensional and multidirectional interaction between trauma, substance use, and spiritual development (i.e. At what point is the individual at in the progression of their substance use? What is the nature of the individual's trauma? Where is the individual in their trauma recovery? What is the individual's understanding and/or experience with religious or spiritual concepts? Do specific ethnic or racial differences moderate the relationship between trauma and spiritual well-being?).

From an administrative perspective, the findings of this study support the need for organizational structures and policies that: (a) reduce gender-specific barriers that limit treatment access; (b) reflect an understanding of the complex clinical needs of women with co-occurring trauma and substance use disorders; (c) support the inclusion spirituality in as part of the treatment paradigm; (d) ensure proactive and ongoing staff development, training and supervision regarding ethical evaluation and implementation of spirituality in service delivery; (e) respect diverse spiritual beliefs; and (f) encourage affiliations that promote and enhance recovery efforts.

Since it is often in the context of counseling that clients begin to explore issues of spirituality, the therapeutic relationship often provides the structure, safety, and support necessary for the exploration of spiritual issues that may promote or impede recovery efforts (Miller, 2003; Atenn & Hernandez, 2004). The findings of this study reinforce the mutuality between a comprehensive trauma assessment that evaluates type of trauma occurrence(s) experienced, the age of the first traumatic occurrence(s), and the frequency of the traumatic occurrence(s) and the individual's level of spiritual well-being. Understanding the complexities and spiritual implications of the trauma history allows the clinician to effectively mobilize spiritual resources that are consistent with the individual's level of spiritual development. For example, in this study, women who had experienced the trauma of sexual molestation had significantly lower Spiritual Well-Being scores than women who had not experienced childhood sexual molestation. Thus the women who had not experienced the trauma of sexual molestation, may exhibit characteristics consistent with Fowler's (1983) stage three or four (spiritual development marked by an ability to engage in non-defensive mutual dialogue with those whose traditions and experiences differ from their own) while those who have experienced childhood sexual molestation may exhibit characteristics consistent with Fowler's stage two or three (spiritual development marked by black and white thinking, rigid adherence "right" or "wrong" spiritual ideologies, and reliance on the guidance of authority figures in formulating their spiritual identity).

Conclusion and Recommendations for Future Research

Substance abuse and trauma symptomology are the most common diagnoses to co-occur among women. Among women in substance abuse treatment, 55% to 95% report a history of trauma (Covington, Burke, Keaton, & Norcutt, 2008; Najavits, et al., 1997). Yet, trauma and addiction are perhaps the two most undiagnosed and misdiagnosed conditions counseling practitioners face (Davidson, 2001; Morgan, 2009; Najavitis, 2004). Frequently, women report the initiation of substance use subsequent to a specific traumatic event in their lives (Tuchman, 2010; Zlupko, Kauffman, & Dore, 1995). A sizeable body of literature has documented the mitigating elements of spirituality in the recovery from co-occurring trauma and substance use disorders. The current study utilized Fowler's (1983) theory of faith development to highlight the developmental aspects of spirituality from a lifespan perspective.

Although advancements have been made in understanding the importance of spirituality in the recovery from co-occurring trauma and substance use disorders, gaps remain in clinically tested, culturally diverse, evidenced-based, gender-specific, trauma-informed models that include spiritually sensitive developmental approaches (Vis and Boynton, 2008). Additionally, comprehensive trauma assessment instruments are limited. The majority of studies use instruments designed to explore symptomatology related to a diagnosed history of PTSD. As a result, there is paucity in the existing literature for women with a history of traumatic occurrences who do not meet diagnostic criteria for PTSD.

References

Adamson, S. J., & Sellman, J. D. (2009). Patient predictors of alcohol treatment outcome: A systematic review. *Journal of Substance Abuse Treatment, 36(1),* 75−86.

Alcoholics Anonymous (1998). *Membership Survey.* New York, NY: General Services Branch, Alcoholics Anonymous, Inc.

American Counseling Association. (2005). *Code of ethics.* Alexandria, VA: Author.

American Society of Addiction Medicine. (2001). *Patient Placement Criteria*, rev. 2nd ed. Chevy Chase, Maryland, American Society of Addiction Medicine.

Anthony, M. M., Orsillo, S. M., Roemeer, L. (2001). *Practitioner's Guide to Empirically Based Measures of Anxiety.* New York; Kluwer Academic.

American Psychiatric Association. (2000). *Diagnostic and Statistical Manual of Mental Disorders, 4th ed.* (DSM-IV). Washington, D.C.: American Psychiatric Association.

Arangua, L., Anderson, R., & Gelberg, L. (2005). The health circumstances of homeless women in the United States. *International Journal of Mental Health, 34*(2), 62-92.

Association for Spiritual, Ethical, and Religious Values in Counseling. (2009, May 5). *Competencies for addressing spiritual and religious issues in counseling.* Retrieved from http://www.aservic.org/competencies.html

Astley, J. (2009). The psychology of faith development. In M. de Souza, L. J. Francis, J. O'Higgins-Norman, & D. Scott (Eds.), *International handbook of education for spirituality, care, and wellbeing* (pp. 231-245). Netherlands: Springer.

Astley, J., & Francis, L. J. (Eds) (1992). *Christian perspectives on faith development.* Leominster, UK: Gracewing; Grand Rapids, Michigan: Eerdmans.

Aten, A. D., & Hernandez, B. C. (2004). Addressing religion in clinical supervision: A model. *Psychology: Theory, Research, Practice, Training, 41*(2), 152-160.

Back, S. E., Brady, K. T., Sonne, S. C., Verduin, M. L., (2006). Symptom improvement in co-occurring PTSD and alcohol dependence. *Journal of Mental Disorders, 194* (9), 690-696.

Back, S. E., Sonne, S. C., Killeen, T. K., Dansky, B. S., Brady, K. T. (2003) Comparative profiles of women with PTSD and comorbid cocaine or alcohol dependence. *American Journal of Drug and Alcohol Abuse*, *29*(1), 169-189.

Beck, A. T., Steer, R. A., & Garbin, M. G. (1988). Psychometric properties of the Beck Depression Inventory: Twenty-five years of evaluation. *Clinical Psychology Review*, 8 (1): 77-100.

Beck, A. T., Ward, C. H., Mendelson, M., Mock, J., & Erbaugh, J. (1961). An inventory for measuring depression. *Archives of General Psychiatry, 4*, 561-71.

Beckman, L. J., & Amaro, H. (1986). Personal and social difficulties faced by women and men entering alcoholism treatment. *Journal of Studies on Alcohol, 47*, 135-145.

Belenky, M., Clinchy, B. M., Goldberger, N. R., & Tarule, J. (1986). *Women's ways of knowing.* New York: Basic Books.

Bloom, B., Covington, S. (1998). *Gender-specific programming for female offenders: What is it and why is it important?* Washington, DC: American Society of Criminology.

Blume, S. B. (1998). Addictive disorders in women. In *Clinical Textbook of Addictive Disorders,* 2nd ed., edited by R. Frances and S. Miller. New York: Guilford.

Blume, S. B. (1988). *Alcohol-dependent women: New insights into their special problems, treatment, recovery.* Minneapolis: Johnson Institute.

Blume, S. B. (1990). Chemical dependency in women: Important issues. *American Journal of Drug and Alcohol Abuse, 16*, 297-307.

Blume, S. B. (1992). Alcohol and other drug problems in women. In J. H. Lowinson, P. Ruiz, R. B. Millman, & J. G. Langrod (Eds.), *Substance abuse* (2nd ed., pp. 852-860). Baltimore: Williams & Wilkins.

Blumenthal, S. (1998). Welcome from the U.S. Public Health Service. In *Drug Addiction Research and the Health of Women: Executive Summary,* edited by C. Wetherington and

A. Roman. Rockville, MD: U.S. Department of Health and Human Services: National

B. Institute on Drug Abuse.

Brady, T. M., & Ashley, O. S. (Eds.). (2005). Wom*en in substance abuse treatment: Results from the Alcohol and Drug Services Study* (ADSS) (DHHS Publication No. SMA 04-3968, Analytic Series A-26). Rockville, MD: Substance Abuse and Mental Health Services Administration, Office of Applied Studies.

Breslau, N., & Kessler, R. C. (2001). The stessor criterion in DSM-IV post traumatic stress disorder: An empirical investigation. *Biological Psychiatry*, 50, 699-704.

Briere, J. (1992). Medical symptoms, health risks, and history of childhood sexual abuse. *Mayo Clinic Proceedings*, *67*(6) 603-604.

Briere, J., & Runtz, M. (1993). Childhood sexual abuse: Long-term sequelae and implications for psychological assessment. *Journal of Interpersonal Violence Special Issue: Research on treatment of adults sexually abused in childhood, 8*(3), 312-330.

Briggs-Gowan, M. J., Carter, A. S., & Ford, J. D. (2012). Parsing the effects violence exposure in early childhood: Modeling developmental pathways. *Journal of Pediatric Psychology*, *37*, 11–22.

Brock, R. N., & Parker, R. A. (2001). *Proverbs of ashes: Violence, redemptive suffering, and the search for what saves us.* Boston: Beacon Press.

Broomer, R. K. (2009). Assessing traumatic event exposure: Comparing the Traumatic Life Events Questionnaire to the Structured Clinical Interview for DSM-IV. *Psychological Assessment, 21*(2), 210-218.

Broomer, R. K., King, V. L., Kidorf, M., Schmidt, C. W., & Bigelow, G. E. (1997). Psychiatric and substance use comorbidity among treatment-seeking opioid abusers. *Archives of General Psychiatry*, 54, 71-80.

Bufford, R. K., Paloutzian, R. F., & Ellison, C. W. (1991). Norms for the Spiritual Well-Being Scale. *Journal of Psychology and Theology*, 19(1), 56-70.

Bureau of Justice Statistics. (2003). *Sourcebook of criminal justice statistics, 2003*, Washington, DC: U.S. Department of Justice.

Campling, P., & Haigh, R. (1999). *Therapeutic Communities: Past, Present, and Future.* London: Jessica Kingsley Publishers.

Cashwell, C., & Young, J. (Eds.) (2005). *Integrating spirituality and religion into counseling.* Alexandria, VA: American Counseling Association.

Cashwell, C. S., Myers, J. E., & Shurts, W. M. (2004). Using the developmental counseling and therapy model to work with a client in spiritual bypass: Some preliminary considerations. *Journal of Counseling and Development, 82*(4), 403- 409.

Center for Substance Abuse Treatment (2005). *Substance abuse treatment for persons with co-occurring disorders.* Treatment Improvement Protocol (TIP) Series, Number 42. DHHS Publication No. (SMA 05-3992). Rockville, MD: Substance Abuse and Mental Health Services Administration.

Chang, B., Skinner, K. M., & Boehmer, U. (2001). Religion and mental health among women veterans with sexual assault experiences. *International Journal of Psychiatry in Medicine, 31*, 77-96.

Chang, G. (1997). Primary Care: Detection of women with alcohol disorders. Harvard Review of Psychiatry *4*(6), 334-337.

Ciarrocchi, J. W., & Brelsford, G. M. (2009). Spirituality, religion, and substance coping as regulators of emotions and meaning making: Different effects on pain and joy. *Journal of Addictions & Offender Counseling, 30,* 24-36.

Clark, C., & Fearday, F. (2001). *Triad Women's Project Group Facilitator Manual and Workbook.* Tampa, Florida, University of South Florida.

Cook, L. S., Epperson, L., & Gariti, P. (2005). Determining the need for gender-specific chemical dependence treatment: Assessment of treatment variables. *American Journal on addictions, 14*, 328-338.

Cole, B., Benore, E., & Pargament, K. (2004). Spirituality and coping with trauma. In S. Sorajjakool & H. H. Lamberton (Eds.), *Spirituality, health, and wholeness* (pp. 49-76). New York: Haworth Press.

Coletti, S. (1998). Service provider/treatment access issues. In D*rug Addiction Research and the Health of Women: Executive Summary*, edited by C. Wetherington and A. Roman. Rockville, MD: U. S. Department of Health and Human Services; National Institute on Drug Abuse.

Compton, W. M., Thomas, Y. F., Stinson, F.S., Grant, B. F. (2007). Prevalence, correlates, disability and comorbidity of DSM-IV drug abuse and dependence in the United States: results from the National Epidemiologic Survey on Alcohol and Related Conditions. *Archives of General Psychiatry*, *64*, 566–576.

Coyle, A. (2011). Critical responses to faith development theory: A useful agenda for change? *Archive for the Psychology of Religion, 33*(3), 281-298.

Courtenay, B. C, Merriam, S. B., & Reeves, P. M. (1999). Faith development in the lives of HIV positive adults. *Journal of Religion and Health, 38*(3), 203-218.

Covington, S. S., Burke, C., Keaton, S., and Norcott, C. (2008). Evaluation of a Trauma-Informed and Gender Responsive intervention for women in drug treatment. *Journal of Psychoactive Drugs, 5*, 387-398.

Covington, S. S. (2000). Helping women recover: A comprehensive integrated treatment model. *Alcoholism Treatment Quarterly, 18*(3), 99-111.

Cowden, M. A. (1992). F*aith development in women: A comparison of the moral development theories of Carol Gilligan and Lawrence Kohlberg and the faith development theory of James Fowler (Gilligan Carol, Kohlberg Lawrence, Fowler James, Women Clergy).* Ph.D. , Temple University.

Cocozza J. J., Jackson E. W., Hennigan K., Morrissey J. P., Reed B. G., Fallot R., and Banks S. (2005). Outcomes for women with co-occurring disorders and trauma: Program-level effects. *Journal of Substance Abuse Treatment, 28*(2), 109–119.

Covington, S. S. (2003). *Beyond trauma: A healing journey for women.* Hazelden.

Covington, S., & Surrey, J. (1997). "*The Relational Model of Women's Psychological Development: implications for substance abuse", Gender and Alcohol: Individual and Social Perspectives*. Sharon Wilsnack and Richard Wilsnack, eds. (New Brunswick, New Jersey, Rutgers Center of Alcohol Studies, pp. 335-351.

Creswell, W.J. (2013). *Research design: qualitative, quantitative, and mixed methods approaches*. (4th ed.). Thousand Oaks, CA: Sage.

Cusack, K. J., Frueh, B. C., & Brady, K. T. (2004). Trauma history screening in a community mental health center. *Psychiatric Services, 55*, 157-162.

Davidson, J.R.T. (2001). Recognition and treatment of posttraumatic stress disorder. *Journal of the American Medical Association, 286*, 584-588.

Davis, T. L., Kerr, B. A., & Robinson-Kurpius S. E. (2003). Meaning, purpose, and religiosity in at-risk youth: The relationship between anxiety and spirituality. *Journal of Psychology and Theology, 31*(4), 356.

Denicola, K. B. (1993). *Manual for faith development research* (rev. ed.). Atlanta, GA: Candler School of Theology.

Denov, M. S. (2004). The long-term effects of child sexual abuse by female perpetrators: A qualitative study of male and female victims. *Journal of Interpersonal Violence, 19*(10), 1137-1156.

Derogatis L. R, & Melisaratos N. (1983). The Brief Symptom Inventory: an introductory report. *Psychological Medicine 13*, 596–605,

Devor. N., (1989). *Toward a relational voice of faith: Contributions of James Fowler's faith development theory, psychological research on women's development, relational feminist theology, and a qualitative analysis of women ministers' faith descriptions.* Boston: Boston University.

Diehl, A. M. (2002). Liver disease in alcohol abusers: clinical perspective. *Alcohol, 27*(1), 7-11.

Dimmitt, J. (1995). Rural mexican-american and non-hispanic white women: Effects of abuse on self-concept. *Journal of Cultural Diversity, 2*(2), 54-63.

Doehring, C. (1993). *Internal Desecration: Traumatization and Representations of God.* New York: University Press of America.

Donleavy, G. (2008). No man's land: Exploring the space between Gilligan and Kohlberg. *Journal of Business Ethics 80* (4), 807–822.

Douglas, A. N., & Jimenez, S. (2008). Ethnic differences in the effects of spiritual wellbeing on long-term psychological and behavioral outcomes within a sample of homeless women. *Cultural Diversity and Ethnic Minority Psychology, 14*(4), 344-352.

Draucker, C. B. (2001). Learning the harsh realities of life: Sexual violence, disillusionment, and meaning. *Health Care for Women International, 22*(1-2), 67-84.

Driedger, S. M. (1997). *Relationships among faith development, ego development, and religious Orientation in HIV+ individuals: A construct validation study.* submitted in partial fulfillment of the requirements for the degree of doctor of philosophy. Siman Fraser University.

Dunn, G. E.; Ryan, J. J., & Dunn, C. E. (1994). Trauma symptoms in substance abusers with and without histories of childhood abuse. *Journal of Psychoactive Drugs 26*, 357-60.

Dykstra, C., Parks, S. D. (1986). *Faith development and Fowler*. Birmingham, AL: Religious Education Press.

Erikson, Erik H. (1980). *Identity and the life cycle*. Vol. 1. W. W. Norton & Company.

Erikson, Erik H. (1968). *Identity, Youth and Crisis.* New York: Norton.

Elhai, J .D., Gray, M. J., Kashdan, T. B., & Franklin, C. L. (2005). Which instruments are most commonly used to assess traumatic event exposure and posttraumatic effects?: A survey of traumatic stress professionals. *Journal of Traumatic Stress, 18*, 541-545.

Elliott, D. E., Bjelajac, P., Fallot, R. D., Markoff, L.S., Reed, B. G. (2005). Trauma-informed or trauma-denied: Principles and implementation of trauma-informed services for women. *Journal of Community Psychology, 33*(4), 461-477.

Elliott, D. M., & Briere. J. (1992). Sexual abuse trauma among professional women: Validating the trauma symptom checklist-40 (TSC-40). *Child Abuse & Neglect, 16*(3), 391-398.

Ellison, C. W. (1983). Spiritual Well-Being: Conceptualization and measurement. *Journal of Psychology and Theology, 11*, 330–340.

Elison, C. W., & Levin, J. S. (1998). The religion-health connection: Evidence, theory, and future directions. *Health Education and Behavior, 25*(6), 700-720.

Enlow, M. B., Blood, E., &Egeland, B. (2013). Sociodemographic risk, developmental competence, and PTSD symptoms in young children exposed to interpersonal trauma in early life. *Journal of Traumatic Stress, 26*, 686-694.

Fallot, R. D. (1997). Spirituality in trauma recovery. In M. Harris & C. L. Landis (Eds.), *Sexual abuse in the lives of women* (pp. 337-355). Amsterdam: Harwood Academic Publishers.

Fallot, R. D. & Heckman, J. P. (2005). Religious/Spiritual coping among women trauma survivors with mental health and substance use disorders. *Journal of Behavioral Health Senices & Research. 32*(2). 215-226.

Falsetti, S. A., Resick, P. A. & Davis, J. L. (2003). Changes in religious beliefs following trauma. *Journal of Traumatic Stress, 16*, 391-398.

Fernhout, J. H. (1986). Where is faith?: Searching for the cote of the cube. In C. Dykstra & S. Parks (Eds.). *Faith Development and Fowler* (pp. 65-89). Birmingham, Alabama: Religious Education Press.

Finkelhor, D., Hotaling, G., Lewis, I., & Smith, C. (1990). Sexual abuse in a national survey of adult men and women: Prevalence, characteristics, and risk factors. Child Abuse and Neglect, *14*, 19-28.

Foa E.B., Cashman L, Jaycox L. (1997). The validation of a self-report measure of posttraumatic stress disorder: *The Posttraumatic Diagnostic Scale*. Psychological Assessment *9*, 445–451.

Fortune, M. (1991). A commentary on religious issues in family violence. Violence in the family: A workshop curriculum for clergy and other helpers. Cleveland, OH: Pilgrim.

Fowler, J. W. (2004). Faith development at 30: Naming the challenges of faith in a new millennium. *Religious Education, 99*, 405-421.

Fowler, J. W. (1981). *Stages of faith.* San Francisco, California: Harper & Row.

Fowler, J. W. (1991). Stages in faith consciousness. *New Directions for Child and Adolescent Development*, *52*, 27-45.

Fowler, J. W., & Dell, M. L. (2006). Stages of faith from infancy through adolescence: Reflections on three decades of faith development theory. In E. C. Roehlkepartai,Wagener, & P. L. Benson (Eds.), The handbook of spiritual development in childhood and adolescence (pp. 34-45). Thousand Oaks, CA: Sage Publications.

Fowler, J., Streib, H. & Keller, B. (2004). *Manual for faith development research* (3rd ed.). Bielefeld, Germany: Research Center for Biographical Studies in Contemporary Religion; Atlanta, Georgia: Center for Research in Faith and Moral Development

Fowler, J. W. & Vergote, A. (1980). Toward Moral and Religious Maturity. Morristown, NJ: Silver Burdett.

Fullilove, M. T., Fullilove, R. E., Smith, M., Winkler, K., Michael, C., Panzer, P. G. and Wallace, R. (1993), Violence, trauma, and post-traumatic stress disorder among women drug users. *Journal of Traumatic Stress*, *6*, 533–543.

Galanter, M., Dermatis, H., Bunt, G., Williams, C., Trujillo, M., & Steinke, P. (2007). Assessment of spirituality and its relevance to addiction treatment. *Journal of Substance Abuse Treatment. 33*, 257-264.

Gall, T. L., Basque, V., Damasceno-Scott, M. and Vardy, G. (2007), Spirituality and the Current Adjustment of Adult Survivors of Childhood Sexual Abuse. *Journal for the Scientific Study of Religion, 46*, 101–117.

Gall, T. L., & *Grant*, K. (2005). Spiritual disposition and understanding illness. Pastoral Psychology, *53*(6), 515-533.

Garbarino, J., & Bedard, C. (1996). Spiritual challenges to children facing violent trauma. *Childhood, 3*(4), 467-478.

Gilligan, C. (1982). *In a different voice: Psychological theory and women's development.* Cambridge, MA. Harvard University Press.

Gill, C. S., Barrio-Minton, C. A. & Myers, J. E. (2010). Spirituality and religiousity: Factors Affecting wellness among low-income, rural women. *Journal of Counseling and Development, 88*(3), 293-302.

Golding, J. M. (1999). Intimate partner violence as a risk factor for mental disorders: A meta-analysis. *Journal of Family Violence, 14*(2), 99-132.

Gomberg, E., & Nirenberg, T., (1993). Atecedents and consequences. In Women and Substance Abuse, edited by E. Gomberg and T. Nirenberg. Norwood, NJ: Ablex.

Gorden, S. M. (2002). Women & addiction: Gender issues in abuse and treatment. Wernersville, PA: Caron Foundation.

Goldberg, R. T., & Goldstein, R. (2000). A comparison of chronic pain patients and controls on traumatic events in childhood. *Disability and Rehabilitation: An*

International Multidisciplinary Journal, 22(17), 756-763.

Golding, J. (1994). Sexual assault history and physical health in randomly selected Los Angeles women. *Health Psychology, 13*(2), 130-138.

Golding, J., Cooper, M., & George, L. (1997). Sexual assault history and health perceptions: Seven general population studies. *Health Psychology, 16*(5), 417-425.

Graham-Bermann, S. A., Castor, L. E., Miller, L. E., & Howell, K. H. (2012). The impact of intimate partner violence and additional traumatic events on trauma symptoms and PTSD in preschool-aged children. *Journal of Traumatic Stress, 25*, 393–400.

Green, C. A., Polen, M. R., Dickinson, D. M., Lynch, F. L., & Bennett, M. D. (2002). Gender differences in predictors of initiation, retention, and completion in an HMO-based substance abuse treatment program. Journal of Substance Abuse Treatment, *23*, 285-295.

Greeno, C. G. & Maccoby, E. E. (1986). How different is the "different voice"? Signs, *11*(2), 310-316.

Grella, C. E., & Joshi, V. (1999). Gender differences in drug treatment careers among clients in the national Drug Abuse Treatment Outcome Study. *American Journal of Drug and Alcohol Abuse, 25*, 385-406.

Greenfield, S. F., Brooks, A. J., Gordon, S. M., Green, C. A., Kropp, F., McHugh, R. K., & Miele, G. M. (2007). Substance abuse treatment entry, retention, and outcome in women: A review of the literature. *Drug and alcohol dependence, 86*(1), 1-21.

Grove, W. M., & Anderson, N. (1982). Simultaneous tests of many hypothesis in exploratory research. *Journal of Nervous and Mental Disease*, 170(1), 3-8.

Gunty, A. L., Frazier, F. A., Tennen, H., Tomich, P., Tashiro, T., & Park, C. (2011). Moderators of the relation between perceived and actual posttraumatic growth. Psychological Trauma: Theory, Research, Practice, And Policy, *3*(1), 61-66.

Hall J. M. (1999). Lesbians in alcohol recovery surviving childhood sexual abuse and parental substance misuse. *International Journal of Psychiatric Nursing Research*, 5(1), 507–515.

Harris, M., Fallot, R. (2001) *Using Trauma Theory to Design Service Systems*, San Francisco, CA: Jossey-Bass.

Harris, M., & The Community Connections Trauma Work Group. (1998). Trauma recovery and empowerment: A clinician's guide to working with women in groups. New York: The Free Press.

Harrison, M., Koenig, H. G., Hays, J., Eme-Akwari, A., & Pargament, K. I. (2001). The epidemiology of religious coping: A review of recent literature. International Review of Psychiatry, *13*(2), 86-93.

Hay, D., Reich, K.H., & Utsch, M. (2006). Spiritual development: Intersections and divergence with religious development. In E.C. Roehlkepartain, P.E. King, L. Wagener, & P.L. Benson (Eds.), The handbook of spiritual development in childhood and adolescence (pp. 46–59). Thousand Oaks, CA: Sage.

Hadzic, Maja. 2011. Spirituality and mental health: current research and future directions. *Journal of Spirituality in Mental Health. 13*(4), 223-235.

Höllinger, F., & Smith, T. B. (2002). Religion and esotericism among students: A cross-cultural comparative study. *Journal of Contemporary Religion, 17*(2), 229-249.

Haynes, C. J. (2009). Holistic human development. Journal of Adult Development, *16*(1), 53-60.

Hee, H. S. (2007). Reflections on the journey of aging Korean Women. In A. M. Brazal & A. Lizares (Eds.), Body and sexuality: Theological-pastoral perspectives of women in Asia (pp. 210-215). Manila: Manila University Press.

Heath, D.B. (1991). Women and alcohol: Cross-cultural perspectives. Journal of Substance Abuse, *3*(2), 175-185.

Heppner, P.P., Wampold, B.E., & Kivlighan, D.M. (2008). *Research Design in Counseling.* (3rd ed.). Hampshire: Cengage Learning.

Herman, J. (1992). *Trauma and Recovery* (2nd ed.) New York: Basic Books.

Herman, J. 1997 (Rev). Trauma and Recovery. New York: HarperCollins.

Hien, D. A., Campbell, A., Ruglass, L. M., Hu, Mei-Chen, Killeen, T. (2010). The role of alcohol misuse in PTSD outcomes for women in community treatment: A secondary analysis of NIDA's Women and Trauma Study. *Drug and Alcohol Dependence*, *111*, 114-119.

Hien, D. A., Cohen, L. R., Campbell, A. N. C. (2009). Methodological innovation to increase the utility and efficiency of psychotherapy research for patient with co-occurring mental health and substance use disorders. *Professional Psychology: Research Practice* , *40*(5), 502-509.

Higgins, A. B., & Follette, V. M. (2002). Frequency and impact of interpersonal trauma in older women. *Journal of Clinical Geropsychology Special Issue: Traumatic exposure and PTSD in older adults*, *8*(3), 215-226.

Hill, P. C., & Pargament, K. I. (2003). Advances in the conceptualization and measurement of religion and spirituality. Implications for physical and mental health research. American Psychologist, *58*, 64–74.

Holcomb, G. L., & Nonneman, A. J. (2004). Faithful change: Exploring and assessing faith development in Christian liberal arts undergraduates. New Directions for Institutional Research, *122*, 93-103.

Hogue, A., Dauber, S., Dasaro, C., & Morgenstern, J. (2010). Predictors of employment in substance-using male and female welfare recipients. *Journal of Substance Abuse Treatment, 38(2),* 108-118.

Issac, S. & Michael, W. (1995). Handbook in Research and Evaluation: A Collection of Principles, Methods, and Strategies Useful in the Planning, Design, and Evaluation of Studies in Education and the Behavioral sciences. (3rd ed.). San Diego, CA: Educational and Industrial Testing Services.

Janoff.Bulman R. (1992). *Shuttered Assumptums: Toward a New Psychology of Trauma.* New York: The Free Press.

Johnson, B. R., Tompkins, R. B., &Webb, D. (2002). Objective hope. Assessing the effectiveness of faith-based organizations: A review of the literature. Philadelphia: Center for Research on Religion and Urban Civil Society, Manhattan Institute.

Juhnke, G. A., Watts, R. E., Guerra, N. S., & Hsieh, P. (2009). Using prayer as an intervention with clients who are substance abusing and addicted and who self-identify personal faith in god and prayer as recovery resources. *Journal of Addictions & Offender Counseling, 30,* 16-23.

Kauffman, S. E., Silver, P. & Poulin, J. (1997). Gender differences in attitudes toward alcohol, tobacco, and other drugs. *Social Work*, *42*, 231-241.

Kendall-Tackett, K., Williams, L., & Finkelhor, D. (1993). Impact of sexual abuse on children: A review and synthesis of recent empirical studies. *Psychological*

Bulletin, 113, 164-180.

Kennedy, J. E., Davis, R. C, & Taylor, B. G. (1998). Changes in spirituality and wellbeing among victims of sexual assault. *Journal for the Scientific Study of Religion, 37*(2), 322-328.

Kerber, L., Greeno, C., Maccoby, E., Luria, Z., Stack, C. & Gilligan, C. (1986). In a Different Voice: An interdisciplinary forum. Signs, 11(2), 304-333.

Kessler, R.C., McGonagle, K.A., Zhao, S., Nelson, C.B., Hughes, M., Eshleman, S., Wittchen, H.U., Kendler, K.S. (1994). Lifetime and 12-month prevalence of DSM-III-R psychiatric disorders in the United States: Results from the national comorbidity survey. *Archives of General Psychiatry, 51*, 8-19.

Khalsa, D. S. (2003). The integration of health and spirituality: Report on a groundbreaking conference. *Total Health, 25*(3), 36.

Kilpatrick, D. G., Resnick, H. S., Saunders, B. E., & Best, C. L. (1998). Victimization, posttraumatic stress disorder, and substance use and abuse among women. In C. L. Wetherington & A. B. Roman (Eds.), Drug addiction research and the health of women (pp. 285-307, NIH Publication No. 98-4290). Rockville, MD: National Institute on Drug Abuse.

Kinney, J. (2000). *Loosing the grip*, (6th edition). Boston, MA: McGraw-Hill.

Koenig, H., McCullough, M., & Larson, D. (2001). *Handbook of religion and health.* Oxford: Oxford University Press.

Kohlberg, L. (1981). Essays on moral development: The philosophy of moral development. (1), San Francisco, CA: Harper & Row.

Kohlberg, L. (1976). Moral stages and moralization. In T. Lickona (Ed.), Moral Development and Behavior, New York: Holt, Rinehart, and Winston.

Kosten, T. R., Kosten. T. A., & McDougle, C. J. (1996). Gender differences in response to intranasal cocaine administration to humans. *Biological Psychiatry*, 39, 147-148.

Kovacs E. J., Messingham K. A. (2002). Influence of alcohol and gender on immune response. *Alcohol Research and Health. 26*, 257–263.

Krystal, H. (1991). Integration and self-healing in post-traumatic states: A ten year retrospective. *American Imago*, *48*(1), 93-118.

Kubany, E. S., Leisen. M., Kaplan, A. S., Watson, S. B., Haynes, S. N., Owens, J. A., & Burns, K. (2000). Development and preliminary validation of a brief broad-spectrum measure of trauma exposure: The Traumatic Life Events Questionnaire. *Psychological Assessment*, *12*(2), 210-224.

Lazarus, R. S. & Folkman, S. (1984). *Stress appraisal and coping*. New York: Springer Publisher Company.

Leufstadius, C., Eklund, M., & Erlandsson, L-K. (2009). Meaningfulness in work: Experiences among employed individuals with persistent mental illness. *Work*, *34*, 21-32.

Levinson, D. J. (1978). The Seasons of a Man's Live. New York: Ballantine Books.

Lidz, V., Sorrentino, D. M., Robinson, L., & Bunce, S. (2004). Learning from disappointing outcomes: An evaluation of prevocational interventions for methadone maintenance patients. Substance Abuse & Misuse, 39(13&14), 2287-2380.

Loft, S., Olesen, K., & Dossing, M. (1987). Increased susceptibility to liver disease in relation to alcohol consumption in women. *Scandinavian Journal of Gastroenterology*, *22*, 1251-1256.

Lucas, L. R., Angulo, J. A., Moal, M. L., McEwen, B. S. and Piazza, P. V. (1998), Neurochemical characterization of individual vulnerability to addictive drugs in rats. *European Journal of Neuroscience*, *10*, 3153–3163.

Luria, Z. (1986). A Methological Critique. In L. K. Kerber, On in a Different Voice: An interdisciplinary forum. Journal of Women in Culture and Society,*11*(2), 316-320.

Mackinley, E. (2005). Understanding the aging process: A developmental perspective of the psychosocial and spiritual dimensions. In F. J. Turner (Ed.), Social work diagnosis in contemporary practice (pp. 213-219). New York, NY: Oxford.

McAdams, D. P. (1993). The stories we live by: Personal myths and the making of the self. New York: Morrow.

McCann, I. L., & Pearlmann, L. A. (1990). *Trauma and the Adult Survivor: Theory, Therapy, and Transformation*. New York: Brunner/Mazel.

McClellan, A. T., Luborsky, L., O'Brien, C. P., & Woody, G. E. (1980). An improved evaluation instrument for substance abuse patients: The Addiction Severity Index. *Journal of Nervous and Mental Disease*, *168*, 26-33.

McGrady, B. S., & Reytek, H. (1993). Women and substance abuse: Treatment modalities and outcomes. In *Women and Substance Abuse*, edited by E. Gomberg and T. Nierenberg. Norwood, N. J.: Ablex.

McHugh, R.K., Rasmussen, J. L., Otto, M. W. (2011). Comprehension of self-report evidenced based measures of anxiety. *Depression and Anxiety*, *28*, 607-614.

McHugo, G. J., Caspi, Y., Kammerer, N., Mazelis, R., Jackson, E. W., Russell, L., Clark, C., Liebschutz, J., Kimerling, R. (2005). The assessment of trauma history in women with co-occurring substance abuse and mental disorders and a history of interpersonal violence. *Journal of Behavioral Health Services & Research, 32*(2), 113-127.

Mendelson, J. H., & Mello, N. K. (1998). Diagnostic evaluation of alcohol and drug abuse problems in women. *Psychopharmacology Bulletin* 34(3), 279-281.

Merriam, S. B. (2007). Transformational leaning and HIV positive young adults. In V. A. Anfara & N. T. Mertz (eds.), Theological frameworks in qualitative research (pp. 23-38). Newbury Park, CA: Sage.

Miller D. & Guidry L. (2001) *Addiction and Trauma Recovery: Healing the Body, Mind and Spirit*. New York: Norton.

Miller, G. (1999). The development of the spiritual focus in counseling and counselor education. *Journal of Counseling & Development, 77,* 498-501.

Miller, G. (2003). *Incorporating spirituality in counseling and psychotherapy.* Hoboken, New Jersey: John Wiley & Sons, Inc.

Miller, W. R. (2002). *Integrating spirituality into treatment*. Washington, DC: American Psychological Association.

Miller, W., & Kurtz, E. (1994). Models of alcoholism in treatment: Contrasting AA and other perspectives with which it is often confused. *Journal of Studies on Alcohol, 55*, 159-166.

Miller, W. R., & Thoresen, C. E. (2003). Spirituality, religion, and health. An emerging research field. *American Psychologist 58*(1), 24–35.

Morgan, R. & Freeman, L. (2009). The healing of our people: Substance abuse and historical trauma. Substance Use & Misuse, *44*(1), 84-98.

Morrissey, J. P., Jackson, E. W., Ellis, A. R., Amaro, H., Brown, V. B., & Najavits, L. M.

(2005). Twelve-month outcomes of trauma-informed interventions for women with co-occurring disorders. *Psychiatric Services, 56*(10), 1213-1222.

Mosley, R. M., Jarvis, D., & Fowler, J. W. (1986). Manual for faith development research. Atlanta, GA: Emory University.

Mumenthaler, M. S., Taylor, J. L., O'Hara, R., & Yesavage, J. A. (1999). Gender differences in moderate drinking effects. *Alcohol Research and Health, 23*, 55-64

Munoz, M., Crespo, M., & Perez-Santos, E. (2005). Homelessness effects on men's and womens health: A comparison between a representative homeless sample and atrisk group. *International Journal of Mental Health, 34*(2), 47-61.

Najavits L.M. & Kanukollu, S. (2005). It can be learned, but can it be taught? Results from a state-wide training initiative on PTSD and substance abuse. *Journal of Dual Diagnosis*, in press.

Najavitis, L. M., Schmitz, M., Gotthardt, S., & Weiss, R. D. (2005). Seeking Safety plus exposre therapy: An outcome study on dual diagnosis men. *Journal of Psychoactive Drugs*, *37*, 425-435.

Najavits, L.M. (2002). *Seeking Safety: a Treatment Manual for PTSD and Substance Abuse.* New York, Guildford Press.

Najavits, L.M., Sullivan, T.P.; Schmitz, M.; Weiss, R.D. & Lee, (2004). Treatment utilization of women with PTSD and substance dependence. *American Journal of Addictions 13*, 215-224.

Najavits, L. M., Weiss, R. D., & Shaw, S. R. (1997). The link between substance abuse and posttraumatic stress disorder in women: A research review. *American Journal on Addictions, 6*, 273-283.

Nason-Clark, N. (1997) That battered wife: How Christians confront family violence. Louisville, KY: Westminster/John Knox Press.

Nason-Clark, N. & Kroeger C. C. (2004). Refuge from abuse: Hope and healing for abused Christian women. Downers Grove, IL: Intervarsity Press

National Drug Intelligence Center (2011). The Economic Impact of Il-licit Drug Use on American Society. *Washington D.C.: United States Department of Justice*. Available at: http://www.justice.gov/archive/ndic/pubs44/44731/44731.

National Institute on Alcchol Abuse and Alcoholism, (2001). Frequently asked questions. Retrieved from www.niaaa.nih.gov/faq/q-a.htm.

National Institute on Drug Abuse (1999). Principles of Drug Addiction Treatment: A Research-Based Guide. National Institute of Health Publication No. 99-4180. Bethesda, MD: National Institute on Drug Abuse. Retrieved from http://www.nida.nih.gov/infofacts/treatmenttrends.html

Niebuhr, H. R. (1951). *Christ and Culture*. New York: Harper and Row.

Nelson-Zlupko, L., Kauffman, E., Dove, M. M. (1995). Gender differences in drug addiction treatment: Implications for social work intervention with substance-abusing women. *Social Work, 40*(1), 45-54.

Neuger, C. C. (2001). *Counseling women: A narrative pastoral approach.* Minneapolis:Fortress. Office of Applied Studies (2002). *The DASIS report: Dually diagnosed female substance abuse treatment admissions: 1999.* Rockville, MD: Substance Abuse and Mental Health Services Administration.

Orsillo, S. M., Raja, S. & Hammond, C. (2002). Gender issues in PTSD with comorbid mental health disorders. In Kimberling P. Ouimette, & J. Wolfe (Eds.) *Gender and PTSD* (pp. 207-231). New York:Guilford.

Orwin R, Francisco L, Bemichon T. (2001). *Effectiveness of Women's Substance Abuse Treatment Programs: A Meta-analysis*. Falrfax, Va: Caliber Associates; NEDS Analytic Summary Series No 21.

Paloutzian, R. F. & Ellison, C. W. (1982). Loneliness, spiritual well-being and quality of life. In L. A. Paplau and D. Perlman (Eds), *Loneliness: A sourcebook of current theory, research, and therapy.* New York: Wiley.

Pargament, K. (2007). *Spiritually integrated psychotherapy: Understanding and addressing the sacred.* New York, NY: Guilford Press

Pargament, K. I., Koenig, H. G., Tarakeshwar, N., & Hahn, J. (2004). Religious coping methods as predictors of psychological, physical and spiritual outcomes among medically ill elderly patients: A two-year longitudinal study. *Journal of Health Psychology, 9*(6), 713-730.

Pargament, K. I. (1997). *The psychology of religion and coping: Theory, research, practice*. New York: The Guilford Press.

Parker, S. (2006). Measuring faith development. *Journal of Psychology and Theology, 34*(4), 337-348.

Pettinati, H. M., Rulstalis, M. R., Luck, G. J., Volpicelli, J., & O'Brien, C. (2000). Gender and psychiatric comorbidity: Impact on clinical presentation of alcohol dependence. *American Journal of Addiction, 9*, 242-252.

Peirce, J. M., Burke, C. K., Stoller, K. B., Neufeld, K. J., & Brooner, R. K. (2009). Assessing traumatic event exposure: Comparing the Traumatic Life Events Questionnaire to the Structured Clinical Interview for DSM-IV. Psychological Assessment, 21(2), 210-218.

Piazza, N. J. (1989). Telescoping of alcoholism in women alcoholics. *International Journal of Addiction*, *24*, 19-28.

Piaget, J. (1970a). Piaget's theory in P. H. Mussen (Ed.), Carmichael's Hadbook of child psychology, *3*(4), 281-199.

Piaget, J. (1970). *Structuralism*. New York: Basic Books.

Prescott, C.A. (2002). Sex differences in the genetic risk for alcoholism. *Alcohol Research & Health, 26*(4), 264-273.

Pritt, A. F. (1998). Spiritual correlates of reported sexual abuse among Mormon women. *Journal of Scientific Study of Religion*, *37*(2), 273-285.

Rahn, C. L. (2008). *Spirituality, religiosity, and trauma in women who have experienced interpersonal violence*. PhD , Azusa Pacific University).

Randall, C. L., Roberts, J. S., DelBoca, F. K., Carroll, K. M., Connors, G. C., & Mattson, M. E. (1999). Telescoping of landmark events associated with drinking: A gender comparison. *Journal of Studies on Alcohol*, *60*, 252-260.

Reinert, D. F., Estadt, B. K., Fenzel, L. M., Allen, J. P., & Gilroy, F. D. (1995). Relationship of surrender and narcissism to involvement in alcohol recovery. *Alcoholism Treatment Quarterly*, *12*(1), 49-58.

Rich, J. M., & DeVitis, J. L. (1985). *Theories of moral development*. Springfield, IL: Thomas,

Richards, P. S., & Bergin, A. E. (2000). *Handbook of psychotherapy and religious diversity*. Washington DC: American Counseling Association.

Ripley, J., Jackson, L., Tatum, R., & Davis, E. (2007). A developmental model of supervisee religious and spiritual development. *Journal of Psychology and Christianity, 26*, 298–306.

Roberts, S. J., Reardon, K. M., & Rosenfeld, S. (1999). Childhood sexual abuse: Surveying its impact on primary care. *AWHONN Lifelines, 3*(1), 39-45.

Ryan, P. L. (1998). An exploration of spirituality of women who survived childhood violence. *Journal of Transpersonal Psychology, 30*(2), 87-102.

Sacks, S. Banks, S., McKendrick, K., & Sacks, J. Y. (2008). Modified therapeutic community for co-occurring disorders: A summary of four studies, *Journal of Substance Abuse Treatment, 34*(1): 112-122.

Scheier, M. F., & Carver, C. S. (1985). Optimism, coping, and health: Assessment and implications of generalized outcome expectancies. *Health Psychology*, 4(3), 219-247.

Schenker, S. (1997). Medical consequences of alcohol abuse: Is gender a factor? *Alcoholism: Clinical and Experimental Research, 2*, 179-181.

Schober, R., & Annis, H. M. (1996). Barriers to help-seeking for change in drinking: A gender-focused review of the literature. *Addictive Behaviors 21*(1), 81-92.

Seybold, K. S. & Hill, P. C. (2001). The role of religion and spirituality in mental and physical health. *Current Directions in Psychological Science, 10*, 21-24.

Selman, R. L. (1980). The Growth of Personal Understanding: Developmental and Clinical Aspects. New York: Academic Press.

Selwyn, P. (1998). Medical and health consequences of HIV/AIDS and drug abuse. In *Drug Addiction Research and Health of Women: Executive Summary*, edited by C

Wetherington and A. Roman. Rockville, MD.: U. S. Department of Health and Human Services: National Institute on Drug Abuse.

Selzer, M. (1971). The Michigan Alcoholism Screening Test: The quest for a diagnostic instrument. *American Journal of Psychiatry, 127*, 1653-1658.

Seng, J. S., Low, L. K., Sparbel, K., & Killion, C. (2004). Abuse-related post-traumatic stress during the childbearing year. *Journal of Advanced Nursing, 46*(6), 604-613.

Serlin, R. C. (1987). Hypothesis testing, theory building, and the philosophy of science. *Journal of Counseling Psychology, 34(4)*, 365-371.

Shaw, A., Joseph, S. & Linley, P. A. (2005). Religion, spirituality, and posttraumatic growth: A systematic review. *Mental Health, Religion, and Culture, 8*(1), 1-11.

Shober, R.& Annis, H.M. (1996). Barriers to help-seeking for change in drinking a gender focused review of the literature. *Addiction Behavior, 21*, 81-92.

Sias, S., (2002) Conceptual and moral development of substance abuse counselors: The relationship to counselor level of education, experience and recovery status. Ph.D. , College of William and Mary.

Silver, R. C., Holman, E. A., McIntosh, D. N., Poulin, M., & Gil-Rivas, V. (2002). Nationwide longitudinal study of psychological responses to September 11. *Journal of the American Medication Association, 288*(10), 1235-1244.

Smetena, I. G. (1984). Morality and gender: A commentary on Pratt, Golding, and Hunter. *Merrill-Palmer Quarterly, 30*(4), 341-348.

Smith, E. J. (2006). The strength-based counseling model: A paradigm shift in psychology. The *Counseling Psychologist, 34*(1), 134-144.

Smith, T. B., McCullough, M. E., & Poll, J. (2003). Religiousness and depression: Evidence for a main effect and the *moderating* influence of stressful life events. *Psychological Bulletin, 129*, 614-636.

Smith, W.C. (1962) *The Meaning and End of Religion*. First Fortress Press Edition 1991.

Snarey, J. (1991). Faith development, moral development, and nontheistic Judaism: A construct validity study. In W. Kurtines and J. Gerwitz (Eds.), *Handbook of moral behavior and development (2)* pp. 279-305.

Stebnicki, M. A. (2006). Integrating spirituality in rehabilitation counselor supervision. *Rehabilitation Education, 20(*2), 115-132.

Steele, P. T. (1999). Relapse and spirituality: Spiritual well-being and quality of life as a critical factor in maintaining recovery from alcohol addiction. Ph.D. , University of Wisconsin-Stout.

Streib, H. (2003). Faith Development Research at Twenty Years. In R. R. Osmer & F. Schweitzer (Eds.), Developing a Public Faith. New Directions in Practical Theology. Essays in Honor of James. W. Fowler (pp. 15-42). St. Louis: Chalice Press.

Sligar, S. R. & Toriello, P. J. (2007). Improving services to clients with addiction issues: New paradigms for vocational evaluation practice. *Vocational Evaluation and Career Assessment Professionals Journal, 4(1),* 17-28.

Smith, D. W., Davis, J. L., Fricker-Elhai, A. E., (2004). How does trauma beget trauma? Cognitions about risk in women with abuse. *Childhood Maltreatment*, *9*(3), 292-303.

Streib, H. (2005). Faith development research revisited: Accounting for diversity in structure, content, and narrativity of faith. *International Journal for the Psychology of Religion, 15*(2), 99-121.

Substance Abuse and Mental Health Services Administration(2013) *Results from the 2012 National Survey on Drug Use and Health: Summary of National Findings*, NSDUH Series H-46, HHS Publication No. (SMA) 13-4795. Rockville, MD: Substance Abuse and Mental Health Services Administration,

Substance Abuse and Mental Health Services Administration. (2011). *Addressing the Needs of Women and Girls: Devleoping Core Competencies for Mental Health and Substance Abuse Service Professionals.* HHS Pub. No. (SMA) 11-4657 Rockville, MD: Substance Abuse and Mental Health Services Administration.

Substance Abuse and Mental Health Services Administration. (2010). *Results from the 2009 National Survey on Drug Use and Health: Volume I. Summary of National Findings* (Office of Applied Studies, NSDUH Series H-38A, HHS Publication No. SMA 10-4586Findings). Rockville, MD: Substance Abuse and Mental Health Services Administration.

Substance Abuse and Mental Health Services Administration. (2007). *Results from the 2006 National Survey on Drug Use and Health: National Findings* (Office of Applied Studies, NSDUH Series H-32, DHHS Publication No. SMA 07-4293). Rockville, MD.

Substance Abuse and Mental Health Services Administration (2006). *Results from the 2005 National Survey on Drug Use and Health: National Findings*. Series H-30, DHHS Publication No. SMA 06-4194. Rockville, MD: Office of Applied Studies.

Substance Abuse and Mental Health Services Administration (2001). *Summary of Findings from the 2000 National Survey on Drug Abuse*. Rockville, MD: U. S. Department of Health and Human Services: Substance Abuse and Mental Health Services Administration.

Sugerman, D. E., DeMartini, K. S., & Cary, K. B. (2009). Are women at greater risk? An examination of alcohol-related consequences and gender. *The American Journal on Addictions*, *18*, 194-197.

Taft, C., Resick, P., Watkins, L., & Panuzio, J. (2009). An investigation of posttraumatic stress disorder and depressive symptomatology among female victims of interpersonal trauma. *Journal of Family Violence*, *24*(6), 407-415.

Taylor, O. D., (2010). Barriers to treatment for women with substance use disorders. *Journal of Human Behavior in the Social Environment, 20*, 393-409.

Thomasson, H.R. Gender differences in alcohol metabolism. In: Galanter, M., ed. *Recent Developments in Alcoholism: Women and Alcoholism*. New York: Plenum Press, 1995. pp. 163–179.

Thompson, S. (1985). Finding positive meaning in a stressful event and coping. *Basic Applied Social Psychology*, *6*(4), 279-295.

Thoresen, C. E. (1999). Spirituality and health: Is there a relationship? *Journal of Health Psycho logy*, *4*, 291-300.

Thorensen, C. E. & Harris, A. H. S. (2002). Spirituality and health: What's the evidence and what's needed? *Society of Behavioral Medicine*. *24*(1), 3-13.

Thurman, R.G. (2000). Sex-related liver injury due to alcohol invoves activation of Kupffer cells by endotoxin. *Canadian Journal of Gastroenterology 14*,129-135.

Tillich, P. (1952) *The Courage to Be*. New Haven, Yale University Press.

Tillich, P. (1957). *Dynamics of faith*. New York: Harper and Row.

Tuchman, E. (2010). Women and addiction: The importance of gender issues in substance abuse research. *Journal of Addictive Diseases*, *29*, 127-138.

U. S. Department of Health and Human Services. (2011). *Treatment Methods for Women.* Rockville, MD: U. S. Department of Health and Human Services, National Institutes of Health, National Institute on Drug Abuse.

U.S. Department of Justice. (1994) *Fact Sheet: Drug Related Crime.* Washington DC: Office of Justice Programs, Bureau of Justice Statistics. Publication No. NCJ-149286.

Van Campen, C. & Cardol, M. (2009). When work and satisfaction with life do not go hand in hand: Health barriers and personal resources in the participation of people with chronic physical disabilities. *Social Science & Medicine, 69 (1),* 56-60.

Van Wormer, K. & Bernes, L. (2004). The impact of priest sexual abuse: Female survivors' narratives. *Affila, 19*(1), 53-67.

Vis, J. & Boynton H. M. (2008). Spirituality and Transcendent Meaning Making: Possibilities for Enhancing Posttraumatic Growth, *Journal of Religion & Spirituality in Social Work: Social Thought, 27*(1-2), 69-86.

Walker, D. F., Reid, H. W., O'Neill, T., Brown, L. (2009). Changes in personal religion/spirituality during and after childhood abuse: a review and synthesis. *Psychological Trauma: Theory, Research, Practice and Policy, 1*(2), 130-145.

Wallen, J. (1998). *Researcher/sex issues.* In Drug Addiction Research and the Health of Women: Executive Summary, edited by C. Wetherington and A. Roman. Rockville, MD: U. S. Department of Health and Human Services: National Institute on Drug Abuse.

Walls, R. T., Moore, L. C., Batiste, L. C., & Loy, B. (2009). Vocational rehabilitation and job accommodations for individuals with substance abuse disorders. *Journal of Rehabilitation, 75(4),* 35-44.

Watlington, C. G., & Murphy, C. M. (2006). The roles of religion and spirituality among African American survivors of domestic violence. *Journal of Clinical Psychology*, 62, 837-857.

Wechsberg, W. M., Luseno, W. & Ellerson, R. M. (2008) Reaching women substance abusers in diverse settings: stigma and access to treatment 30 years later. *Substance Use Misuse*. *43*(8–9),1277–1279.

Wiechelt, S. A., Miller, B., Smyth, N. J., & Maguin, E. (2011). Associations between post-traumatic stress disorder symptoms and alcohol and other drug problems: Implications for social work. *Practice: Social Work in Action, 23*(4), 183-199.

Weinberger, A. H., McKee, S. A., Mazure, C. M. (2010). Inclusion of women and gender-specific analyses in randomized clinical trials of treatments for depression. *Journal of Women's Health, 19*(9), 1727-1732.

Weisner, C. & Schmidt, L. (1992). Gender disparities in treatment for alcohol problems. *Journal of the American Medical Association, 268*, 1872-1876.

Weiss, S.R., Kung, H.C., & Pearson, J.L. (2003). Emerging issues in gender and ethnic differences in substance abuse and treatment. *Current Women's Health Report, 3*, 245-253.

West, S. L. (2008). The utilization of vocational rehabilitation services in substance abuse treatment facilities in the U.S. *Journal of Vocational Rehabilitation, 29*, 71-75.

Westermeyer, J. & Boedicker, A. E. (2000). Course, severity and treatment of substance abuse among women verses men. *American Journal of Drug and Alcohol Abuse, 26*(4), 523-535.

Westgate, C. E. (1996). Spiritual wellness and depression. *Journal of Counseling & Development, 75*, 26-35.

White, J. M., Wampler, R. S., & Winn, K. I. (1998). The Identity Style Inventory: A revision with a sixth grade reading level (ISI-6G). *Journal of Adolescent Research, 13*(2), 223-245.

White, K. A., Brady, K. T., & Sonne, S. (1996). Gender differences in patterns of cocaine use. *American Journal on Addictions, 5*(3) 259-261.

Wiechelt, S. A. (2008). Introduction to the special issue: International perspectives on Women's *Substance use. Substance Use & Misuse*, 43, 973-977.

Wilke, D. (1994). Women and alcoholism: How a male-as-norm bias affects research, assessment and treatment. *Health & Social Work*, *19*, 29-35.

Woods, J. (1998). Translating basic research into the clinical setting. In *Drug Addiction Research and the Health of Women: Executive Summary*, edited by C. Wetherington and A. Roman, Rockville, MD: U. S. Department of Health and Human Services: National Institute on Drug Abuse.

Young, N. K. (Consensus Panel Chair) (2000). *Integrating substance abuse treatment vocational services*. Treatment improvement protocol (TIP) series 38. U.S. Department of Health and Human Services. DHHS Publication No. (SMA) 00-3470. MD: Rockville. Retrieved from http://ncadi.samhsa.gov

Zankowski, G. L. (1987). Responsive programming: meeting the needs of chemically dependent women. Alcoholism Quarterly, *4*,53-66.

www.ingramcontent.com/pod-product-compliance
Lightning Source LLC
LaVergne TN
LVHW090405210926
848480LV00002B/460